Trauma and Pastoral Care

A Ministry Handbook

Carla A. Grosch-Miller

CANTERBURY
PRESS
Norwich

© Carla A. Grosch-Miller 2021

Published in 2021 by Canterbury Press
Editorial office
3rd Floor, Invicta House,
108–114 Golden Lane,
London EC1Y OTG, UK
www.canterburypress.co.uk

Canterbury Press is an imprint of Hymns Ancient & Modern Ltd
(a registered charity)

Hymns Ancient & Modern® is a registered trademark of
Hymns Ancient & Modern Ltd
13A Hellesdon Park Road, Norwich,
Norfolk NR6 5DR, UK

Scripture quotations are from the New Revised Standard
Version of Bible © 1989 by the Division of Christian Education
of the National Council of the Churches of Christ in the USA.
Used by permission. All rights reserved.

British Library Cataloguing in Publication data

A catalogue record for this book is available
from the British Library

978-1-78622-333-3

Typeset by Regent Typesetting
Printed and bound by
CPI Group (UK) Ltd

Contents

Part 3: The Changing Story of Life and Faith

Appendices

List of Figures

For those whose lives are upended by trauma
and for those who care

Introduction

I started writing this book in March 2020 just as Covid-19 sparked a radical national response in the United Kingdom. Places of worship closed, all but key workers were sent home, and social distancing (compassionate spacing of two metres) was instituted. All of this aimed to halt the spread and flatten the curve of infection, steward National Health Service resources and save lives. I continued to write as the pandemic unfolded. Its presence as a conversation partner will be apparent in the pages that follow.

The idea for the book had been around for a few years as I worked with an outstanding team of researchers and educators on congregational trauma (http://tragedyandcongregations. org.uk). That work culminated in the publication of an academic text, *Tragedies and Christian Congregations: The Practical Theology of Trauma* (Warner et al. 2019), and teaching curricula for ordinands, clergy, lay leaders and people with oversight of ministers. That work and this book were funded by Grant TWCF-0185 from the Templeton World Charities Foundation, Inc., to whom we are very grateful. The views expressed here are those of the author and should not be taken to reflect the views of the Foundation.

Writing in the midst of a pandemic proved a tonic some of the time and was very challenging at other times. Engaging in purposeful activity during a crisis helps reboot and calm the nervous system. But Covid-19, which is in another league in terms of its complexity, required reserves of energy and clarity that can be in short supply in times of trauma and chronic stress. Alongside writing, I worked with our team to create and deliver training sessions on trauma-informed ministry to support clergy and others to survive, adapt and reflect. At the time I also was serving as part-time transitional (interim) minister to a congregation that had come through a difficult time before the pandemic. Covid-19 extended my call and we weathered it together. The confluence of three strands of pandemic-related work proved a rich resource.

The field of traumatology is fairly new. While psychiatrists sought to understand and help 'hysterical' women in the late nineteenth century and war veterans during and after the two world wars, it was not until after the Vietnam War that considerable resources began to be focused on understanding the nature of trauma. Returning combatants and people who had survived rape provided a tragic pool of human experience to study. Once brain imaging became available in the 1990s, the field took off. By the early part of the twenty-first century, even biblical scholarship was seized by an interest in how trauma had impacted and formed the sacred texts. Soon thereafter trauma theologies were being written and discussed.

This book seeks to gather together in an accessible way fundamental insights about trauma that have been generated in the last 30 or so years, so that they may inform and strengthen our ability as church ministers, leaders and volunteers to care for traumatized people and communities. It is a holy task that requires our best thinking and caring.

How to use this book

The chapters are short and clearly titled so that you can dip in and out as needed. The lay of the land is this: Part 1 focuses on the physiological impact of trauma on the individual, the minister's role particularly at the moment of impact and the power of resonant care. Part 2 introduces collective trauma and discusses pastoral and liturgical strategies over the long haul. Part 3 explores making narrative and theological sense of tragedy and how we might cultivate resilience. I close with an Afterword that contemplates the possibility of rolling complex collective traumas as we live on into the Anthropocene. There are Appendices that provide additional resources.

If you are in the midst of a traumatizing event, I suggest you read the first chapter (Trauma and the Brain) to get a grounding in what trauma does in the individual. Another particularly helpful chapter to notice is Chapter 3 (Rapid Response) which includes a Trauma Response Toolkit to use in the immediate moment when the terrible thing happens to a congregation or community. Chapter 8 (The Hurting Whole) shares a 'phases of collective trauma response' chart from the Institute for Collective Trauma and Growth (US) that may help you orient where you and your church may be in the aftermath of a tragedy. Because the post-traumatic journey is long and challenging, self-care is not an optional extra: read Chapter 7 (Superheroes).

Acknowledgements

This book is the product of the work, insight and wisdom of a number of people. I want particularly to acknowledge the exceptional trauma team I mentioned earlier: Professor Christopher Southgate, the Revd Hilary Ison and Dr Megan Warner. This book would not exist but for the grantsmanship and encouragement of Professor Southgate. Our team was assisted by the support, insight and skill of Constellations Supervisor and Trainer Lynn Stoney, Practical Theologian Dr R. Ruard Ganzevoort in the Netherlands, Dr Kate Wiebe, Director of the Institute for Collective Trauma and Growth in the United States, the members of our Advisory Board (Professor John Swinton, Dr Ruth Layzell, the Revd Dr Roger Abbott, Dr Sarah Horsman of Sheldon Lodge and Dr Wiebe), our interviewees (you know who you are – we couldn't have done this without you), the contributors to *Tragedy and Christian Congregations*, and our many students. A special thank you goes to my illustrator the Revd Kathy O'Loughlin, a skilled pastor and priest who has been a companion on the journey, and to the Revd Thom M. Shuman who shares his World Communion

Liturgy in the time of pandemic (Appendix G). Finally, I want to thank St Andrew's United Reformed Church, Monkseaton, who provided the opportunity for me to put flesh on words and theories. I am grateful to have been able to seek to practise what I teach and preach with such a responsive and caring congregation.

A health alert

In our study of trauma, we quickly learned that even reading about trauma can trigger a trauma response. If you experience discomfort or distress while reading this book, it may be that you are experiencing a triggered traumatic response. One of the key texts in this area is titled *The Body Keeps the Score* (van der Kolk 2014). Our bodies hold the imprint of traumatizing events of which we may have no conscious memory. Triggered responses include a racing heartbeat; feelings of anxiety, threat, confusion or distress; a brain that has gone offline. This is entirely normal. If something like that happens, just notice it gently and warmly. Acknowledge that something is happening and speak kindly to yourself. Plant your feet on the ground, take slow deep breaths, do some small movement of your hands, draw your attention to your physical surroundings. Phone a friend. The good news is that what we learn about trauma in the context of congregational or community-wide events gives us tools to help navigate the personal tragedies that are part of every human life.

PART I

The Traumatized Individual

I

Trauma and the Brain

To be human is to be vulnerable. To be vulnerable is to be able to be wounded (from the Latin *vulnus* – wound). We always need one another, but when we are wounded the need is even greater. From the beginning, Christian ministry has included tending to broken bodies, hearts and spirits. Many in ministry find this part of our vocation to be particularly rewarding and occasionally very challenging. The intent of this book is to equip and to encourage those who tend to the wounds to self, others and communities that arise from traumatizing events.

The word *trauma* comes from the Greek and refers to things that can wound, hurt or defeat a person. Take a moment to make a mental list of those things that have the potential to wound, hurt or defeat a person, a congregation or a community. The list may include things you or those you know have experienced.

Your list will no doubt include natural disasters – flood, earthquake, tsunami, fire – as well as events that have human involvement – acts of violence (murder, suicide, terrorist attacks, injury), betrayals of trust, church closure. It will include death, perhaps the death of a child or of significant church members, and serious illness or the threat of illness such as that occasioned by pandemics. The climate crisis and economic dislocation are candidates too. Whether the traumatizing event is global or personal, its impact on individuals, families and communities can be profound.

Look at your list. What are you feeling in your body as you contemplate having these land on the doorstep of your church or community?

It is likely you are feeling anxious, perhaps a bit overwhelmed. Notice how your body reacts to the feeling. Are your shoulders tight or your neck in a knot? Your heart rate accelerated? Your stomach churning? Your legs restless? Each one of us will have particular bodily responses that put us on alert. Learning to listen to your body and read your own responses is one of the tools it is helpful to cultivate or further develop. As we progress you will see why.

This chapter will explain what is happening in the brain of an individual who is traumatized by an event. While traumatic responses vary widely among individuals, the basic neuroscience is the same. The brain responds instantly in order to maximize the chance that the individual will survive. By understanding what is happening in the brain and body, we can fine tune caring responses.

The language we use in common parlance is not particularly helpful. People name a flood or a fire as traumas. But the *trauma is not the event itself.* Rather it is in the brain's response to the event. Trauma is the response generated when our capacity to adapt is overwhelmed. Peter Levine (1997, p. 197) describes life as a stream flowing between two banks. As events good and bad happen, you adapt oscillating energy up and down as needed, doing what you can to go with the flow and stay afloat. But when something big happens – when the flood, the fire, the act of violence comes – something too much, too soon, too fast for your normal coping mechanisms to respond, the energy bursts the banks and the brain does what it can to save your life: it propels you to flee or to fight. If neither of those is possible, you will become immobilized (freeze or flop and drop) while a natural anaesthesia floods your body.

In short, we are hard-wired for survival. It is all in the brain.

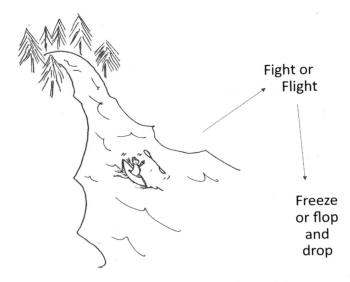

Fight or
Flight

Freeze
or flop
and
drop

Figure 1: Fight, flight or freeze or flop and drop

The three-part brain

Since the 1960s it has been hypothesized that the human brain reflects our evolution as a species and its development in an individual person's life (MacLean 1990). We can think of the brain as having three parts: the *autonomic nervous system* (the reptilian brain), the *limbic system* (the mammalian brain) and the *neocortex* (the neo-mammalian brain). Given the innumerable interconnections within the whole brain, this three-part model is a gross oversimplification. But it helps us to understand what happens when an overwhelming event strikes.

The *autonomic nervous system* (ANS), which we share with lizards and snakes and which develops in humans in the womb, regulates the bare necessities, the things our bodies need to be doing to stay alive: breathing, eating, sleeping, waking, feeling discomfort and pain, digestion, and ridding the body of toxins through urination and defecation. If you hold your hand up before you with the palm facing you,[1] you can visualize the ANS above the wrist as the brain stem, the wrist as the base of

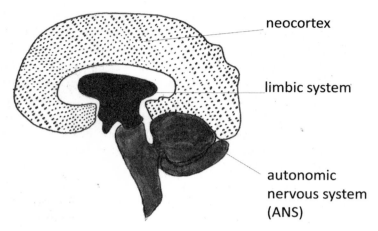

neocortex

limbic system

autonomic
nervous system
(ANS)

Figure 2: The three-part brain

the skull and beginning of your spinal cord, and the forearm as its continuation and a nerve superhighway. The ANS connects the skull brain (the hand) to the rest of the body. Information flows up and down (more up than down, as we shall see). The ANS is called autonomic because it is automatic. We don't have to think about breathing or digesting – we just do it.

Sitting directly above the brain stem is the hypothalamus. Together they control the energy levels of the body, coordinate the heart and lungs, and seek to keep the endocrine (hormone secretion) and immune systems in a relatively stable balance. Again, we do not have to think about any of this to make it happen.

The hypothalamus is part of the *limbic system*, which we share with otters and elephants and which is organized primarily in the first six years of human life. All animals that nurture their young and live in groups share this brain development. Here is the command-and-control post for living in the world with others. It is at the root of our motivation and our emotional life including our parenting and reproductive behaviour and contains the warning and response system for danger that will keep us alive. Central to the limbic system is the amygdala: two almond-shaped clusters of nuclei that are the distant early warning system of the brain, scanning the environment every 12 to 100 times a second asking *Am I safe? Do I belong?* (Peyton 2017, p. 26). The amygdala works with the hippocampus – an organ involved in memory – to quickly identify whether what is presently being experienced may be life-threatening or comparable to dangerous or difficult past experiences. Here is a first clue as to why individuals respond differently to potentially traumatizing events: we each have had different life experiences that shape our nervous system responses. Our culture and context also shape our perceptions of threat and danger.

Bessel van der Kolk (2014, p. 57), a key figure in the field of traumatology and the author of *The Body Keeps the Score*, calls the two more primitive parts of the brain – the ANS and the limbic system – the 'emotional brain'. It is at the heart of our central nervous system, noticing danger or special opportunities (e.g. for love) and releasing the appropriate hormones.

Using the hand model of the brain, hold your hand up in front of you, leaving the fingers open, and press your thumb into the middle of your palm. The thumb represents the core elements of your limbic system: the amygdala, hypothalamus and hippocampus.

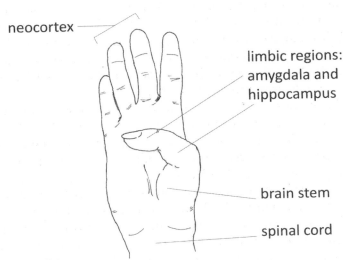

neocortex

limbic regions:
amygdala and
hippocampus

brain stem

spinal cord

Figure 3: The hand model of the three-part brain

When the amygdala senses danger it sends rapid fire messages to the hypothalamus to call for the release of stress hormones (including cortisol and adrenaline) that will enable the brain-body to defend against the threat. Our heart rate increases as does our blood pressure and breathing. At the same time but more slowly the neocortex will be alerted. By the time we realize we may be in danger our body has already begun to respond. The flood of stress hormones will send us into fleeing or fighting. In extreme or chronic trauma, if neither flight nor fight is possible, we will freeze or flop and drop, becoming unable to act. Immobilized, our bodies also secrete natural opioids that limit the experience of pain and may induce a trance-like state.

Once the danger passes, the body resumes normal functioning fairly quickly for most people, depending on the nature and extent of the event and on the state of their nervous system. Chapter 4 (Reboot) offers ways to facilitate recovery of normal function. But for a small number of people, particularly those who have experienced chronic or extreme trauma in the past, the brain-body can get stuck in a trauma response and remains on high alert or numb.

Let me reiterate here that the trauma response is the entirely normal, life-saving response of our brain-bodies. We have no control over these physiological responses. There is no shame in being traumatized, in running away or being frozen. The oldest parts of our brain have taken over so that we may survive. We have no choice about whether to be traumatized or what specific traumatic response happens.

The emotional brain is the first to interpret the sensory input from our environment and our bodies. This input goes into the thalamus where it is processed and passed on to the amygdala (the early warning centre) at lightning speed to interpret its emotional and physical significance.

The third part or level of the brain, the *neocortex*, receives the information more slowly. Its function is to perform a more conscious and nuanced interpretation of what is going on in and around us. The neocortex is the top or outer layer of the brain. It takes up about 76 per cent of total brain volume. Our neocortex is thicker than that of other primates and includes the prefrontal lobes which make it possible for us to think, plan, use language, anticipate, empathize, imagine, create, and also to stop ourselves from doing something harmful or inappropriate. This part of the brain develops last in an individual and because of neuroplasticity – the brain's ability to form new neural connections to adapt or compensate – it continues to change throughout our lives.

To represent this level of the brain, hold up your hand with your thumb pressed into your palm and fold down your four fingers so that every part of the hand is connected to every other part. The four fingers are the neocortex; all three parts of the brain are connected. In a normal non-traumatizing situation, sensory input comes in, is processed by the emotional brain, and the neocortex weighs in on the situation. That said, the power of our emotional brain is such that it impacts a great deal of our behaviour – impacting what we eat, who we befriend and who we choose as a partner, what we like (to see, hear, do) and what we hate. Our emotions give us essential information about the value of our experiences to us, which can inform our use of reason. We are not and never will be entirely 'rational' creatures.

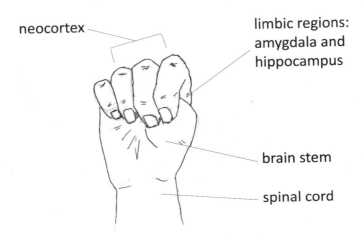

Figure 4: *The hand model of the brain*

In extremis the emotional brain takes over with its lifesaving flood of stress hormones and the neocortex is cut off. Using the hand model fling your fingers open. When traumatized we 'flip our lids' so that we can quickly get out of the situation, resist it or become immobilized and anesthetized. The whole brain is no longer functioning together as the emotional brain takes over. The strength of our trauma response will depend on the perceived severity of the danger. The more intense the reaction of our emotional brain, the less connected and able our thinking brain is to influence what is happening.

Van der Kolk (2014, pp. 64–5) uses an analogy given by Paul MacLean (the developer of the three-part brain model) for the relationship between our thinking brain and our emotional brain as being akin to the relationship between a relatively competent rider and their unruly horse. When things are going well (smooth enough path, decent weather), the rider is in control. But put a snake on the path or lightning in the sky and all hell breaks loose as the horse bolts and the rider is left clinging to the saddle. When a person's amygdala perceives danger, or when they are seized by strong emotion (fear, rage, sexual desire), the thinking brain is no longer in control or in dialogue with the emotional brain. We act on instinct.

This knowledge helps us to understand our own behaviour. When we are greatly emotionally impacted by something, we are less likely to think or act rationally. We are less empathetic. We are less creative. Our neocortex blocked or inhibited, we may say or do things that we later regret.

The individual is unique

The same potentially traumatizing event will have a different impact on the individuals in its ambit. This is for two basic reasons. The first I have alluded to: our individual nervous systems are unique. They are the product of our genetic inheritance and our life experience – what we are born with and what happens to us. We are born with the basic equipment, which may carry our ancestors' traumatization through epigenetics.

Our life experience (pre- and post-birth) impacts the behaviour of our genes and the shape and responsive patterns of our limbic system as it develops in the first six years of our lives. If our experience is one of safety and nurture, our baseline will be more towards calm and openness. If our experience is of abuse or neglect, we will be more familiar with experiencing fear and responding to abandonment or threat.[2] Later experiences will continue to impact our limbic systems – we are not locked into one way of being. Trusting, caring relationships heal and resource us, just as further abuse and stress make us more susceptible to a trauma response. If we have lived with chronic or severe trauma, our nervous systems may be hypervigilant and readily triggered or we may be numb to the world, constricted in our ability to respond.

The second reason for individual variability is that trauma is about the loss of meaningful things. A manufacturing plant closes. For one person the loss of a job brings freedom and opportunity – they hated that job and have been plotting an escape. For another, redundancy deprives them of essential income or a sense of identity. The first individual is not traumatized; the second person may be. The context and meaning of the event determine whether it will be traumatizing. We could see this during the first phase of the Covid-19 pandemic. For some the lockdown was a gift; they had an assured income and welcomed the respite from a pressured life while managing the anxiety of witnessing increasing infections and deaths. For others, the lockdown resulted in a loss of income or the ability to be with a sick or dying loved one. For these people and for those who lost loved ones, the pandemic was more likely to engender a traumatic response.

What trauma does

The trauma response is a whole-body response with several specific outcomes. With the neocortex cut off, Broca's area in the left frontal lobe – one of the speech centres of the brain – is disconnected. We may lose our ability to put thoughts or feelings into words. We shall see later (Chapters 10 and 12 on lamentation and liturgy) the usefulness of ritual action when words fail us. In trauma it is very difficult to organize one's experience into a story that makes sense, yet it is just that sense-making that will be key to recovery in the long-term.

The difficulty of sense-making is partly due to the impact of trauma on the hippocampus in the limbic region of the brain. The hippocampus is a key centre for learning and memory in the brain. It is involved in the consolidation of short-term memory into long-term memory. Having worked with the amygdala to communicate danger, the hippocampus is then impacted by the flood of stress hormones and no longer able to store and integrate information. As a result the imprint of a traumatic experience is a collection of sensory and emotional traces: pictures, sounds and physical sensations with no organized, coherent story of what happened. This explains how a sound or a smell or a glimpse of something from the corner of the eye can trigger a trauma response if it is tangentially similar to the original offending event. In those moments time is suspended and the individual is re-experiencing the trauma as though it were present.

The traumatic response interrupts the story of who we are and severs us from our body-selves and our resources. We will not know if we are hungry or thirsty or have to go to the toilet. We will not have the rational capacity to connect with resources we have accumulated over our lifetimes. Until our nervous system begins to calm, we are lost and cut off from what we will need to recover.

Finally, a tragic event shatters our assumptions about how the world should be. Every time I bury the child of a living parent I say, 'This is not right.' It is not; children should outlive their parents. Our mental world is held together by a framework of assumptions that enable us to live and function with our vulnerability: that there is sense and order in the world; that the world is benevolent and safe and there is meaning and purpose to life; and that we matter (see Chapters 8 and 9). When senseless things happen, when the earth itself or other people become a danger and we are under threat, our assumptions shatter. It will be some time before we will be able to pick up the pieces and weave again a meaningful framework and story that integrates what has happened into our lives.

Signs of trauma response

How can we tell if someone is traumatized? Traumatic stress responses can include exhaustion, confusion, inability to concentrate, sadness, anxiety, agitation, anger, numbness, dissociation, physical arousal and blunted affect. People may also experience symptoms associated with Post-Traumatic Stress Disorder (PTSD):[3] intrusive re-experiencing of aspects of the event, avoiding anything resonant with the event, and hyper- or hypo-vigilance. Most traumatic stress responses are normal; they affect most survivors and are socially acceptable, psychologically effective and self-limited. As we will see in Chapter 4 (Reboot) the nervous system recalibrates and returns to normal for most people within four to six weeks.

Delayed traumatic reactions – common among clergy and first responders – include unrelenting fatigue, sleep disorders, nightmares, fear of recurrence, anxiety focused on flashbacks, depression and avoidance of emotions, sensations or activities that are even remotely associated with the traumatizing event. Clergy and responders are also at risk for vicarious or secondary trauma: see Chapter 7 (Superheroes).

There may be some people – 5 per cent or fewer of survivors of an event – who will experience more severe trauma responses as their nervous systems get stuck in hypervigilance without periods of relative calm or rest, or they dissociate and are cut off from the living. They may experience intense intrusive recollections; their brain perceives that the event is still happening despite the fact that they are physically safe. Persistent trauma stress responses may be symptoms of PTSD. This group of sufferers is best served by mental health workers trained in trauma work.

For those of us in leadership in communities of faith, the reality of the trauma response and impact will shape how we think, plan, care and lead in the days, weeks and months to come.

Is a pandemic a traumatizing event?

We know that because of the unique nature of each individual's life experiences and resources, the Covid-19 or any pandemic will elicit trauma responses in some people. Their adaptive capacity will be overwhelmed and their emotional brains will take charge. That is to be expected. Perhaps that partially explains the panic buying of hand sanitizer, toilet rolls and more food than could be eaten at the start of Covid-19. As regards individuals, Bessel van der Kolk observed that the early weeks of the pandemic presented 'pre-traumatic' conditions such as lack of predictability and connection, immobility and the loss of safety.[4] But can the pandemic itself be considered a trauma?

A week after the UK first declared that non-essential workers should stay at home due to Covid-19, a group of theologians gathered on Zoom to discuss what was happening and how to support ministers and churches. We pondered the question of whether the pandemic was a collective trauma. There was no doubt that what we had learned about trauma, how it upends life and shatters assumptions and what kinds of pastoral responses work, could be applied usefully to the outbreak. As the weeks and months went by, it was clear that the pandemic would affect our physical and economic lives dramatically in the short term and for a long time after. I will say more about pandemics and other global events as complex collective trauma in Part 2 (Collective Trauma).

Further reading

Steve Haines (2016) with artist Sophie Standing has created a clever little comic book explaining what trauma is, how it changes the way our brains work and how we can overcome it.

Key takeaway points

- Trauma is a physiological response to a perceived threat when a person's adaptive capacity is overwhelmed (too much, too fast, too soon).
- When we are in danger the more primitive parts of our brains take over and our thinking brain is cut off.
- This is a life-saving phenomenon and nothing to be ashamed of.
- The traumatized person is cut off from their resources and their assumptions about how life should be are shattered.
- Not all people will be traumatized by the same event.
- Each individual's trauma response is unique, shaped by their physiology and life experience and the meaning of the event.
- Clergy and first responders to crisis events are susceptible to delayed trauma responses as well as vicarious or secondary trauma.

Notes

1 Dr Daniel Siegel devised the hand model of the brain. He demonstrates and explains it at 'Dr Dan Siegel's Hand Model of the Brain', *YouTube*, 9 August 2017, https://youtu.be/f-m2YcdMdFw, accessed 13.12.2020.
2 It is beyond the scope of this book to cover developmental trauma incurred in infancy or childhood.
3 Post-Traumatic Stress Disorder was first listed in the *Diagnostic and Statistical Manual of Mental Disorders* (DSM), the official list of mental disorders recognized by the American Psychiatric Association, in 1980 in the DSM-III. This came about through the combined advocacy of rape survivors and Vietnam veterans. The PTSD entry continued to

change as new editions of the DSM were published to reflect growing understanding. Symptoms generally fall under categories of re-experiencing the original traumatic event, hyperarousal or numbing and avoidance. See www.nhs.uk/conditions/post-traumatic-stress-disorder-ptsd/symptoms/, accessed 1.01.2021.

4 van der Kolk, Bessel, 'When the COVID-19 pandemic leaves us feeling helpless', *National Institute for the Application of Behavioural Medicine*, www.nicabm.com/when-covid19-leaves-clients-feeling-help less/, accessed 13.12.2020.

2

Trust Your Gut, Discern Your Role

Responding to a traumatizing event or traumatized people calls for careful attention to what is happening in one's own body, as well as to what is happening to other people and in the world. Cultivating the ability to tune into what our bodies know – our 'felt sense' – helps us to respond in the best way possible under difficult circumstances.

The gut instinct and the 'felt sense'

From an early age I lived in my head. It is a pretty interesting place, but it has not served me as well as I hoped. For one thing, I continue to find unexplained bruises on my arms, legs and hips and have no idea how they got there, although I do have vague memories of moments of painful impact. More importantly I did not learn how to trust my gut – to hear what my body is telling me and to know what to do with that information. So I said *yes* to every invitation, inadvertently committing myself to overwork and over-commitment regardless of the cost. It was not until I hit the wall and crumbled, having experienced a cascade of traumatizing events, that I began at least to try to hear. For the last few years I have made a conscious effort to be in my body, attend to its needs and listen to it. Life has been transformed for me.

One of the members of the ace trauma team I work with, Hilary Ison, is trained in systems constellations and group work. Hilary is keenly aware and tuned in to how our bodies know things that we do not often realize, and that we can trust our gut. In this chapter I will be relying in part on her chapter in *Tragedies and Christian Congregations* (Ison 2019), on Bessel van der Kolk's *The Body Keeps the Score* (2014) and on Sarah Peyton's *Your Resonant Self* (2017).

Our bodies know a lot more than we realize. We know when someone is standing too close to us and when they are too far away. We sense people's feelings – in themselves and about us. We know when we've offended and when we've delighted.

In the previous chapter I talked about the limbic system being key to how we live in the world with others. We are a pro-social species. In theological terms we talk about being made in and for relationship with others and look to the Trinity for the model perfection of that reality (distinctive persons in relationships of mutuality and love). In neurobiological terms we flourish when we are in harmonious, caring relationships with others. Infants thrive and develop when they are attended to, fed and touched. So do adults. One of the most powerful things I learned in our study of trauma is that we literally are made for love.[1] That is a theological statement of the highest order. During the Covid-19 pandemic, the loss of social contact – of seeing people's faces and of reaching out to touch or be touched – was deeply problematic for many and led to increased mental health problems. It also led to some creative ways of connecting with others. People put teddy bears in their windows for children to count, pinned up rainbows in appreciation of key workers, and met in gardens and on streets while keeping compassionate distance. We know our need of connection with one another.

Our bodies are designed to provide us with information about ourselves in a social world. Here is how the felt sense works in the brain-body.[2] Look again at our hand model of the brain (see Chapter 1): hand up and facing you, thumb pressed against the palm and fingers closed around it. The brain stem is wrist level. From the brain stem descends the parasympathetic and sympathetic nervous systems which make up the autonomic nervous system. The sympathetic nervous system speeds us up for action and is involved in the fight or flight response. The parasympathetic nervous system slows us down. It includes the longest nerve in the body: the vagus nerve. The word *vagus* derives from the Latin for 'wanderer'; the vagus nerve wanders through the body connecting the brain to the heart, lungs, stomach and intestines. It is the 'rest and digest' nerve, linking the head brain to the enteric brain, the complex system of about 500 million sensory and motor neurons embedded in our gastrointestinal walls (Peyton 2017, p. 162). We tend to think that the flow of information in our bodies is primarily downwards from the head to the body. But 80 per cent of the information flow through the vagus nerve is from the body up into our head brain (Peyton 2017, p. 135). Our gut-based information enables the brain to do its job of assisting 'rest and digest' and also impacts our behaviour whether we are conscious of it or not. We speak of knowing things 'in our gut'. That is literally true.

The gut as a source of knowledge is nothing new. The ancient Greeks located the seat of emotions in the bowels, as did biblical writers who in particular located compassion there.[3] It seems the ancients intuitively knew that the enteric brain was an important source of information.[4]

Cultivating our felt sense – our capacity to tune into what our bodies know – is a skill that serves us well. The signs will be different for all of us. The task is to learn to recognize the body sensations that underlie our emotional reactions. We may learn the signs of anxiety and threat as we feel our heart rate rise and chest or neck tighten, our hands clench or our legs stiffen. We may read the clench in our belly as a warning, or the warm glow rising up our necks to our cheeks as embarrassment. The deep sigh of contentment. The tightening of shoulders. Involuntary movements give us clues. Our felt sense enables us to know what enhances our well-being and what enables our creativity and goodness. It also alerts us to what is more death-dealing than life-giving and to what will not serve our wholeness or authenticity. We can trust the information; it tells us about where we are in the moment.

But can we always trust the information from our felt sense? Might it lead us astray? In this area trusting the information means listening to it and working with it. We accept what our body is telling us. What we do in response to that information is our choice after we have brought our thinking brain into the conversation. For instance, my body might be telling me that I am attracted to another person. Bringing my thinking brain into the conversation enables me to think through the consequences of acting on those feelings, what the attraction might be about (we can be attracted to people who have some quality we want or who remind us of a significant other) and to choose how to respond in line with my values and commitments.

To work with our felt sense the first step (*sensing*) is to notice and to accept what we are feeling – kindly, without judgement and without trying to change or rush to interpret. Just notice. Simply noticing what we are feeling brings it into awareness and can begin a shift in it as tension is released. It is as if our body, which has been trying to get our attention, begins to relax when it finally has it. The next step is to *name* what we are feeling.[5] This enables further release and acceptance. When an emotional experience has not been acknowledged or named, it remains in the body. Neuroimaging has shown that sensing and naming soothe and regulate our emotional brain. This kind of mental process also stimulates the creation of new neural pathways that strengthen the connection between the emotional and rational brains, building our capacity to self-regulate. When we name what we are sensing and feeling, it is surfaced and we can work with it by taking the next step: asking *what do I need?*

I recently inadvertently used this process aloud with my husband. I was getting ready to travel to deliver trauma training to an august group and feeling quite anxious – my tummy was churning and my shoulders were tight (sensation). I told David that I was anxious (naming). He reminded me that I am an experienced educator and that I know my stuff; I got this. It was just what I needed: to remember who I was and what I was capable of, and to be willing simply to offer what I had without anxiety about how I might be received. David's comment connected me to myself and my resources.

How does connecting to the felt sense relate to leading in a time of trauma? When the terrible thing happens we are thrown into the deep end, thrashing about for a life preserver.

We may be traumatized ourselves, or if not traumatized in a state of high alert and responsiveness. We need all the help we can get, connecting to what is in our heads, our hearts and our bodies. The first task will be to seek calm – breathing deeply and slowly will activate the vagus nerve and bring oxygen to all parts of our brain-body.[6] Doing whatever we can that helps us to relax will enable us to connect to our resources. If we are able to do it, tuning into our felt sense, naming what is going on and asking what we need will equip us for the moments, hours, days and weeks to come.

Discerning your role

The next chapter provides a Trauma Response Toolkit which includes a checklist of what to do when a terrible thing happens in your congregation or community. The first thing on the list is to breathe and to pray. Take a deep breath or three, lengthening the exhale as that is most calming. Pray in whatever way works best for you. Prayer is a bridge to the deepest, truest resource we have. Opening an empty space to be present to God and to yourself – for five or ten minutes – will keep you from reacting too quickly and help you to connect to your resources.

The second task is to discern the role that you should take in responding to the crisis. It is highly likely if you are a minister that you will feel it is necessary to immediately dive in and take the lead. *People will be expecting it of me*, your emotional brain will think. *This is what I am here for.* Take a breath; you need to think this through with your whole brain.

Years ago, while researching clergy sexual misconduct, I read that a significant number of ministers are narcissistically wounded (Churches Together in Britain and Ireland 2002, p. 88). We seek the admiration of others in order to shore up our feelings of inadequacy; we need to be needed. I winced when I read this. But it is good to be reminded that our motivation for acting may be about more than we think. Often there will be many motives at work, some more helpful than others. Sometimes we act out of our own need to be affirmed, in charge or needed. That may not serve the needs of the congregation or community.

The truth is that you may not be the right person to lead the charge. If you have been recently bereaved, if you have suffered a trauma in the past which is triggered by current events, if you have ill health or a family situation that will be significantly adversely impacted, or for any number of other potential reasons, you may not be able to give the quality of leadership that the situation calls for. There is no shame in that; it is just fact. If that is the case, you need to recognize it and prepare a Plan B. To choose not to lead the response may be one of the most difficult decisions you have ever made. You need to be connected to all of your resources to make it: your felt sense, your rational knowing, those who are closest to you.

If you discern that you are not the person to be leading the charge, the next task is to discern who is, be it an individual or a small group, and what other role(s) you may play. Only you know your gifts, capabilities and limits. Find the role that plays to your strengths and minimizes the possibility of harming others because of your limits. The road ahead will be long and challenging and you want to be able to fulfil your promises if possible. Then begin to build the response team, communicating the roles you envision people taking in order to rise to meet the needs and opportunities of the moment.

Key takeaway points

- Some 80 per cent of the information flow about how we are in our bodies and in the world and what we are feeling comes up from the gut (enteric brain).
- We can cultivate our felt sense to receive and evaluate some of this information as a helpful resource.
- We tune into and work with our body's information when we notice our bodily sensations, name what we are feeling and ask what it is that we need.
- In a time of crisis we must discern our role, listening to our felt sense, our rational brains and trusted resources.

Notes

1 Being made for relationship is held in tension with the need to be a unique self. Family systems theory holds that the two fundamental life forces are to be an 'I' with agency and identity and to be part of a 'We', to belong. These two forces are held in tension with individuals coming to different balances between the 'I' and the 'We', called self-differentiation. For the application of family systems theory to congregational life, see Edwin H. Friedman, 1985, *Generation to Generation: Family Process in Church and Synagogue*, New York and London: The Guilford Press.

2 The concept of the 'felt sense' comes from Eugene Gendlin, 1981, *Focusing*, New York: Bantam Books, quoted in Levine (1997, p. 67).

3 The Greek word translated 'compassion' in contemporary English literally meant 'to be gutted': e.g. Matthew 9.36, Matthew 20.33–34, Mark 8.1–2, Luke 7.13, Luke 10.33, Luke 15.20. Thanks to an anonymous commentator on the Sheldon Hub in response to a video interview I did in October 2020, www.sheldonhub.org/forums/forum/thread/5157. The Sheldon Hub is an online community hosted by Sheldon, a community offering specialist care for people in ministry.

4 You may enjoy listening via BBC Sounds to *The Gut Instinct: A Social History*, episode 3 'The Language of the Gut', released on BBC 4 on 26 December 2018. Written and presented by Tim Hayward, produced by Rich Ward, featuring lexicographer Susie Dent, accessed 16.10.2020.

5 If you have difficulty naming your feelings, try Geoffrey Roberts's *Feelings Wheel*, https://imgur.com/gallery/tCWChf6, accessed 20.04.2020. Choose a central feeling, then home in on more subtle nuances by moving to the next ring and choosing two that capture more specifically what you are feeling. Do that again with the outer ring.

6 Other means of stimulating the vagus nerve include humming, singing or chanting in a low resonant tone, gargling, cold water face immersion and restorative yoga poses that include slight backbends, forward bends or twists. Healthy eating contributes to vagus nerve activity. See '15 ways to stimulate your vagus nerve to improve gut health', *Neomed Institute of Wellness and Rehabilitation*, www.neomedinstitute.com/blog/15-ways-to-stimulate-your-vagus-nerve-to-improve-gut-health, accessed 13.12.2020.

3

Rapid Response:
Trauma Response Toolkit

The Trauma Response Toolkit below is also Appendix A in the back of this volume; a Word copy can be found on our website (http://tragedyandcongregations.org.uk). The front page has a grid for information you will need close to hand when the terrible thing happens. You will note that the last cells ask for your social media details. This is because there is the possibility that you will not have access to your office computer, server, tablet or phone and will need to be able to send out and receive information from someone else's device. Complete the front page of the toolkit at your earliest convenience. You may wish to place it in a resource bag that will also include water, a snack, a Bible, hand sanitizer, tissues and a high visibility vest. Place the bag where you (and only you) will have easy access to it in case of emergency.

The back page of the Toolkit has a checklist of things to consider when the terrible thing first happens and is unfolding before your eyes, followed by a briefer list for after the acute phase. The second list will make more sense after you read Part 2 of the book on Collective Trauma. Please note that responding to a traumatizing event is very context dependent. If a step on the list does not apply to your situation, skim to see if there is any applicable wisdom, disregarding the irrelevant parts. Similarly, as experienced at times during the Covid-19 pandemic, some actions may not be possible for legal or public health reasons. Consider the principles implicit in the advice and seek to meet the goals in diverse ways. For instance, if physical gathering is not possible, consider other means of gathering such as via the internet.

TRAUMA RESPONSE TOOLKIT

Preparation *prior to* disaster

	Contact name	Contact details
Regional Denominational Head Office		
Church Staff		
Key Church Lay Leaders (including emergency contacts)		
Denominational Media Contact		
Local Police		
Local Disaster Response		
Plumber		
Electrician		
Town Councillor/Mayor		
Ecumenical Partners		
Interfaith Partners		
Mental Health Providers (trauma-aware)		
Social Media details (for remote access)		

Put together a resource bag with water, a snack, a Bible, hand sanitizer, tissues, a high visibility vest and this completed form where you can grab it on the way out the door.

During the acute phase:

- Take a deep breath; pray – connect to yourself and God
- Discern your role
- Call your regional office; negotiate who will communicate with the media
- Alert your support people
- Call your lay leadership; assemble a response team – what can we offer?
- Identify circles of impact
- Distinguish between urgent and important
- Open the church; rally the troops
- Consider gathering the congregation or the public, in collaboration with other faith community partners and local agencies
- Create an information system
- Check in with church members and others
- Create a press-free zone?
- Care for the carers/consider debriefing for first responders

Remember: This heroic phase will be followed by a difficult period of disillusionment. Pace yourself; make self-care a priority so that you can lead through the days, weeks and months ahead.

After the acute phase:

- Watchful waiting as a pastoral strategy
- Welcome honest expression of feelings; do not sugar-coat reality
- Re-establish normal worship and meeting schedule if possible
- Consider whether any special events would be helpful
- Remind the congregation we are on a journey that will last some time
- Draw on rich resources in our Bible and tradition
- Care for the carers
- Care for self; arrange supervision or coaching
- Schedule holiday leave

Helpful resources

Tragedy and Congregations Website (UK): http://tragedyand
congregations.org.uk/
Institute for Collective Trauma and Growth (US): www.ictg.
org/
The Sheldon Hub – doing healthy ministry together: www.
sheldonhub.org/

Unpacking the Trauma Response Toolkit

During the acute phase

- Take a deep breath
- Discern your role

The previous chapter addressed the first two items on the list.
Recall what you have learned about the brain: trauma cuts
us off from our resources. The more you can do to calm and
collect yourself, the better access you will have to all your
resources and the better able you will be to discern your role
and follow the rest of the checklist.

- Call your regional office; negotiate who will communicate
  with the media

When a terrible thing happens, one of your primary roles
is to connect yourself and others to resources that will help
you respond. Your regional denominational office (diocese,
Synod, circuit superintendent, regional minister) is one of
those resources. They need to know what is happening in your
patch so that they can back you up and provide resources such
as pastoral support and media advice. Terrible things attract
media attention. Having someone shove a microphone into
your face can be both intimidating and seductive. In the heat
of the moment (remember, your emotional brain will be firing
on all cylinders with your thinking brain lagging behind), it

will be easy to say something that can be used out of context or that you later regret. In the immediate aftermath of a devastating event that included the death of many, a reporter shoved a microphone into a minister's face and asked what it felt like. The minister responded honestly, 'It's exhilarating!' And it was. There was an outpouring of support and high heroics in response to the tragedy; the minister was witnessing humanity at its best and had purposeful work to do. But you can imagine how this comment played on the airwaves. So one of the decisions to make in that first phone call is who will be the media contact. There may be people in the office who are trained for this. At one step removed they will be able to provide measured and thoughtful commentary to journalists. Having one voice speak for the church is a wise and useful policy.

• Alert your support people

This will take less than two minutes. Send a quick text or email to people you know will hold you in prayer and be a listening ear when you need it. Tell them briefly what is happening, ask for prayer and discretion, and ask them to check in with you at the end of the day. Just do it. You will not be thinking about how to take care of yourself in the coming hours and you will be too tired at the end of the day to reach out. Having someone away from the frontline supporting you with prayer and watching out for you will help you to bring your best to the tasks ahead over the coming days.

• Call your lay leadership; assemble a response team – what can we offer?

We must not do this work alone. Another key resource is your lay leadership. If or when you have time, assemble a small response team. If you are meeting virtually or physically begin with a centring moment and prayer. Your calm, less anxious presence will help them to connect to their resources. The Trauma Response Toolkit checklist can provide the items of your agenda. The prime question is: What can we offer to meet people's immediate needs?

- Open the church; rally the troops

In a time of crisis people instinctively know that they need to gather. Our limbic systems, geared as they are to relating to others, seek the confirmation and assurance of others. If it is possible, open the church building. Churches have incredible resources for times such as these: physical space, high volume tea-making facilities, rotas of volunteers and set-apart sacred spaces that have held human sorrow and joy for generations. We have a deep knowledge of the movement of the soul and the power of ritual to contain confusing, painful and difficult feelings. Our buildings have been markers of something special in our communities sometimes for hundreds of years. They hold memory and signal hope. People who would not darken a church's door in ordinary times may be drawn into the sheltering space of a church in a time of need.

Alan Everett, priest of St Clement and St James Church of England near Grenfell Tower, reflected that on the night of the 2017 fire,

> ... opening the church and switching on lights were the most significant things I've ever done as a priest. It encapsulated everything I've ever stood for in terms of trying to create light and trying to open doors; I felt as though my entire ministry as a priest was encapsulated in those few minutes, but it wasn't just about me ... I was representing the ministry of this church going back for 150 years.[1]

As the tragedy unfolded the church found itself pouring cups of tea, offering a listening ear, being a repository for donated goods and doing innumerable other necessary tasks in service to the community.

The closure of churches during certain phases of the Covid-19 pandemic meant that church leaders and communities were cut off from a primary resource, a loss that was felt deeply by many.

- Identify circles of impact

To get a handle on what needs to be done, draw a set of concentric circles. In the middle put the names of those most immediately impacted ... those whose lives, safety, health and well-being are most directly affected. Work your way outwards adding the names of those less directly affected. Identify what if anything you can do for any of these people and consider what would be the best use of your resources. Be aware that people who have been recently bereaved or experienced other traumas may be more vulnerable to a traumatic response to events even if they would ordinarily be in an outer circle.

Consider what other resources (local agencies, charities, ecumenical and interfaith partners) may be available and how you may cooperate. It is essential not to impede whatever disaster relief work may be going on. You may be able to offer resources that assist or complement what others are doing.

Trauma fragments individual lives, families and communities as it shatters the assumption that the world is ordered and benevolent. Working with others not only prevents wasteful duplication of energy but also sends an implicit healing message of unity and human kindness.

- Distinguish between urgent and important

As you consider what you can do, what resources are available and what you will commit to, distinguish between urgent and important. At impact and in the moment everything seems important, and it may well be. But some things are urgent and need to be attended to first. *Safety is of prime importance.* There is a fundamental rule among those in the life-saving business: never put yourself in a position to be a casualty.[2] While seeking to provide safety for others do not put yourself or others in harm's way. The next urgent matters concern the basic provisions necessary for life – shelter, water, food.

While safety and basic provisions may be provided by others, the church may have special capacity to provide the next tier of human need: offering care and a sense of belonging. Being present in a warm and caring way to those who are suffering in the immediate aftermath of a tragedy will minimize later suffering in the long run. See the next two chapters, 'Reboot' and 'Care that Heals', for more on care.

- Consider gathering the congregation or the public, in collaboration with other faith community partners and local agencies

Public gathering events such as vigils enable people to be together in a way that provides a container for the frightening emotions that will be running rampantly through the community. Such events can be pulled together quickly; simplicity is your friend. Intentional moments of silence and singing are calming. People who sing together breathe together and heart rates begin to slow. Lighting and holding a candle becomes an act of defiance against the disorder of the event and an act of solidarity with all who are suffering. The power of numerous small lights to dispel darkness cannot be underestimated.

Again, collaborate with others. This is not a competition for who gets in first with healing strategies. Rather, it is an opportunity to work together for the common good, holding and beginning to stitch together the torn social fabric. A number of the clergy we interviewed as part of the Tragedy and Congregations project spoke of how helpful it had been to have built up relationships with local agencies and businesses and other faith communities (Christian and non-Christian) in the years before the crisis. Relationships of trust made communication and collaboration smooth; people on the end of a telephone line or email were known human beings. Difficult issues could be more readily acknowledged and negotiated. In a flood, worship spaces were shared. In a terrorist attack, the local authority reached out to religious communities to provide events that helped the community to come together in grief and live out their connection with each other. After a fire, communities of faith provided services that local agencies were unable to muster. All the while individuals and communities experienced the collaboration as reassurance and hope.

At the event, allow for the full expression of the depth of pain. Now is not the time to explain or assure that all will be well. People need to be allowed to be where they are, to feel what they are feeling. When pain and confusion are acknowledged, they slowly begin to recede. In your own communications honest struggling is ultimately more healing than cosmetic cheeriness. Music may provide a container for difficult feelings, as may silence. Recall that trauma impacts a speech centre in the brain; symbolic actions have great power to express otherwise inexpressible feelings of sadness, grief and hope.

A word about the placement of temporary memorials: you do not want this event to be the defining event in church life for a long time to come. Make a space – a paper wall, a memorial book – for notes to be left. If flowers are left, let them be placed where it will be natural to move them respectfully later on (e.g. where the Christmas tree goes). When the time comes to move memorial items it can be done sensitively and publicly in a way that honours victims and survivors.

• Create an information system

In a crisis people need information. The provision of clear, reliable information is part of a healing strategy that enables people to calm themselves and begin to set reasonable expectations and develop coping strategies. It also has the benefit of decreasing the opportunity for unhelpful gossip or rumour to spread. The police and some media outlets are useful and reliable sources of public information. During the Covid-19 pandemic, the UK government regularly provided updated information on the BBC.

There are terrible things that happen where information will not be readily forthcoming. For instance if the minister is accused of sexual or financial misconduct or anything that will trigger criminal or disciplinary procedures, the congregation will not be given full information while the investigation is ongoing. This is necessary to protect the integrity of the legal proceedings. In such matters, best practice is to invite a police officer, social worker or lawyer to address the congregation and share general information, explaining why specific information cannot be shared and speaking to what generally happens and what kind of information may be available in the future.

• Check in with church members and others

Early on, devise a system for checking in on how the individuals in your congregation are coping. If the trauma is ongoing, regular check-ins help people feel connected. You may also have regular church building users or hirers who will appreciate some kind of acknowledgement of the difficulty of the present time and offers of care. Some church users may be more vulnerable than others depending on the reason for their groups and may require additional thought and care – for instance groups for people with learning difficulties, bereavement groups, and mums and tots' groups.

• Create a press-free zone?

If the media are present you may wish to rope off a part of your church or garden and post a sign saying 'Press-free Zone'. Most journalists will respect it. This will enable people in grief to be free of the thrust microphone and intruding camera. Given the ubiquitous presence of mobile phones with cameras you may want to consider another sign saying 'No Photos Without Permission'.

• Care for the carers

Decide how you will exercise care for your volunteers on the front line of responding to people in distress. It will be distressing and exhausting to pour endless cups of tea, witness the impact of the event, listen and care. Do not let anyone work more than eight to twelve hours in a day. Check in with how they are feeling; acknowledge their contribution with gratitude. Send them home if they look like they need a rest. And set a good example. You yourself will need rest and care to be able to lead your congregation over the days, weeks and months that it will take to recover. Vicarious and secondary trauma responses are real things to watch for; see Chapter 7 (Superheroes).

Remember too that clergy and first responders are prone to function well in the moment but later suffer delayed trauma reactions. Share that information with your front line so that they know what to expect. Appendix B is a document prepared by the Revd Dr Roger Abbott for Response Pastors, the disaster response wing of Street Pastors. This is sent home with each volunteer at the end of every session of service.

Key takeaway points

- Before a crisis, fill out page 1 of the Trauma Response Toolkit and place it in a bag with emergency supplies.
- In a crisis, pull out the Trauma Response Toolkit checklist and follow it.

Notes

1 The Revd Alan Everett, interview with the Tragedy and Congregations team. See also A. Everett, 2018, *After the Fire: Finding Words for Grenfell*, Norwich: Canterbury Press.

2 One of the deeply disturbing aspects of the Covid-19 pandemic early on was the lack of adequate personal protection equipment (PPE) for key workers who were required to have close contact with people who were or might have been infected with the virus. This resulted in deaths of NHS staff and care workers, public transport workers and others.

4

Reboot

You have opened the church, mustered a rota of volunteers, fired up the kettles and invited all and sundry into your sacred space. What will work now for people who stumble in, traumatized and hurting or numb?

Steve Haines (2016, pp. 26–7) offers an OMG – *Orient, Move, Ground* – strategy for people in the acute phase of a traumatizing incident or for people who are experiencing strong triggered responses. To *orient* the survivor, help them to connect with the physical place and the people around. Give warm eye contact; be your calmest, best self as you invite them to sit or grab a cup of tea. Your warmth and calm will help the survivor's nervous system to begin to calm. Draw their attention to something physical – the hardness of the chair, the number of empty teacups on the table, light coming through a stained-glass window, anything that engages the senses.

Move also encourages connection with the body. When a person is traumatized, their body may get stuck in an action of fight or flight that was unable to be completed. Haines advises to start by encouraging small movements – toe wiggles, pushing one's legs into the floor, rubbing the hands. He says that 'we contract in fear to make ourselves small, we expand and move forwards when we feel safe – so practice expanding' (Haines 2016, p. 27). Even imagining that we are running on the beach calms the nervous system. When we move, agency hormones such as serotonin are activated and metabolize the stress hormones that have been flooding the traumatized brain-body. The simplest of acts, from eating and drinking to going to the toilet, help metabolize those hormones. This work of agency hormones explains in part why bystanders rush to help out in the aftermath of a traumatizing event: we instinctively know that doing something will help calm us.

Finally, *ground* connects a person to their body by focusing on physical sensation. Invite the survivor simply to report the details of safe, specific sensations: *I can feel the ground beneath my feet, the chair holding me up, my clothing against my skin* ... The more detailed the better. What happens inside the survivor's brain-body is that, as they begin to inhabit the present moment and their bodies feel safety, the nervous system calms.

Do not be surprised if the survivor is shaking. Shaking is a natural mechanism – we literally shake off fear, releasing tension. Normalize what is happening for the person. Notice the shaking; thank the tremors for doing the work of helping to reboot the nervous system.

Remind people that trauma reactions are completely normal and natural. They are how the human brain-body acts to ensure our survival. Most people (80 per cent or more) will recover normal functionality in four to six weeks as their bodies metabolize the stress hormones and the nervous system is rebooted. Some 15 per cent may need some help to process what they have experienced. For the roughly 5 per cent who get stuck in intrusive, hypervigilant or numbing responses beyond six weeks, trauma-sensitive professional assistance may be required to break the cycle and recalibrate the nervous system (Jackson 2017, p. 28). It is not necessary or helpful in the immediate aftermath to share these statistics (remember, the neocortex has flipped its lid) but it is helpful to normalize what is happening – to say, *What you are experiencing is entirely normal for what you have just been through.*

The National Health Service England's advice for immediate post-traumatic treatment is *watchful waiting*[1] which enables people to recover through their natural coping mechanisms and systems of support. You will be familiar with this if you watch police dramas on the television: after giving terrible news the officer asks if there is someone that they can call. The officer is connecting the person to their resources; those resources will be grounded in trusting and caring relationship. Connecting people to their own resources strengthens those resources and builds resilience in the individual.

Church listeners can assure people that it is entirely normal to have strong, even disturbing reactions after a traumatizing event. They can listen with warmth and compassion while encouraging people also to connect with friends and families about what they have experienced. Not everyone will be able to talk about what happened in the aftermath of a trauma and encouraging people to talk could be re-traumatizing. It has to be the right time and the right person. The mantra in trauma recovery work is this: *the survivor is the expert*. A pastoral carer's primary task is to be present to the traumatized person, to normalize their responses, to 'hear them into speech'[2] if that is what they need, and to connect them to their resources.

The good news is that ordinary human care is powerful medicine in a traumatizing situation. We do not have to be experts in trauma to care. We just need to be warm and present and to do the things that church people do: pay attention to what's going on; telephone, text and email; offer a meal or a lift. Ordinary human care is more effective, robust and sustainable than grand gestures. And it does not depend on clergy or lay leaders. It is the role of the baptized and follows Jesus' new commandment (John 13.34). We love one another.

Focus on needs

The first focus of our immediate care is basic needs. No one can begin to recover from anything until they are assured that their physical survival is not at stake. Consider Abraham Maslow's hierarchy of human needs.

Water, food, shelter and safety are basic. Once we have assured that those needs are met, we turn to the emotional and psychological needs that enable a person to stabilize, reboot and recover after a traumatizing event. The OMG strategies described above are part of establishing an inner sense of safety. Love and belonging are met by caring presence that facilitates comfort, consolation, rest and reunion with loved ones.

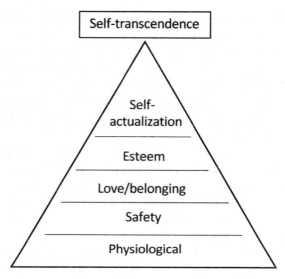

Figure 5: Maslow's hierarchy of needs

Here it is important to consider the power of physical contact. A hug conveys safety and belonging to those who want them. When we are hugged, our brains release endorphins, which are a natural defence against emotional distress (Jackson 2017, p. 26).[3] We feel cared for and valued in a time of fragmenting chaos and loss. It is an embodied connection. But, and this is a big but, some people are repelled or even further traumatized by touch; a hug could have the opposite effect of calming consolation. We need to be watchful, tune into our felt sense and read the clues, not assuming that touch will be welcome or helpful. There is no harm in asking *Do you need a hug?*

Late in his life, Maslow added self-transcendence above self-actualization (Koltko-Rivera 2006, p. 306). He recognized that beyond the healthy individual who has become fully themselves, there are those who become better human beings for others as well as themselves. Maslow's addition resonates with contemporary studies of happiness, which relate personal happiness to giving to others (Park et al. 2017).[4] Self-giving and loving neighbours as ourselves is fundamental for Christians. This is underscored by the neuroscience that tells us that human beings are relational creatures. And it relates to a later task in post-traumatic recovery which is that of meaning-making. You will recall that trauma is attended by the loss of meaning. Once people's nervous systems are rebooted, attention begins to turn to the meaning of what has happened: how to make sense of the events and finding purpose and life in the aftermath. I will say more about this in Part 3, The Changing Story of Life and Faith.

Before turning to a more considered reflection on the kind of care that heals, how does what we have learned so far apply to ongoing and developing crises like pandemics?

Rebooting during a pandemic

As I noted at the end of Chapter 1, at any time during a pandemic there will be individuals who are hardest hit and may be traumatized through the serious illness or death of a loved one, the loss of a job or business, or other aspects of the lockdown or pandemic. Rebooting strategies absolutely apply to them in the immediate aftermath of the traumatizing event, as well as to those for whom the pandemic triggers traumatic responses. Whenever people are hyper-aroused or numbed, showing the signs of a traumatic response, OMG strategies can be used to help calm or reboot their nervous systems.

The interesting question that we are living through at the moment is, assuming that the pandemic is also a complex collective trauma, how does society reboot? What enables us to start to calm or engage the collective nervous system so that it can begin to engage more of its brain power to respond helpfully and constructively?

The pandemic is all about the body: the vulnerability of our individual bodies to a virus for which we have no immunity; the preservation of the health and life of individual bodies; the integrity of the body politic as it seeks to preserve life and to protect and utilize national resources to meet the challenge of mass illness and death; the trust of individual bodies in the body politic. Applying OMG to the body politic we see the immediate intense focus of government activity as it *orients* to the threat to human life posed by the virus, instituting stay at home measures that are widely and repeatedly communicated. *Movement* occurs in the mobilization of resources to meet the basic needs of people: medical resources are stewarded and a push for more resources made; food distribution and transport workers are denoted essential services; wage provision for 'non-essential' workers and funds for small and medium businesses are made. The focus on infection and death rates *grounds* the government response in the physical reality of the virus's impact on human bodies. And amid all this serious business, social media and interpersonal communication is awash with care, connection, courage and creativity, often with a humorous or beautiful bent. I laughed more and was moved to tears more often during the first lockdown than I had before or after. Standing in the front door, clapping and whooping for the NHS, care and other essential workers on Thursday nights at 8pm, I often had to wipe away the moisture forming at the corners of my eyes. Reading and re-circulating emails and Facebook posts both silly and meaningful gave me joy (I'm particularly fond of talking dogs). Innumerable online video conferencing (thank you, Zoom) put virtual flesh on words and sustained important life-giving connections. The pain of polarization over Brexit melted away as people came together to fight Covid-19. It was a beautiful thing. Sadly, as we will explore in Part 2, it was not meant to last. The early responses to crises like pandemics are unifying and heroic, and ultimately unsustainable (see Chapter 8). The lessons of the early phase, however, may be retained.

If there is anything the pandemic reinforced particularly in the early days, it was that we are indivisible from one another. The human bond between people and the bonds between humanity and the whole creation are indissoluble. Those bonds can be forgotten (Brown 2018a) but they cannot be broken. It is my most fervent hope and prayer that as threat and danger fade, we will remember and begin to organize our lives and our life together in ways that respect these bonds.

Ostensibly, then, the government responded to the pandemic

to enable the calming of the body politic. The acute attention to the reality of the body and its vulnerability, with all that means, enabled its response. And bodily practices of care and connection, laughter and tears kept us afloat.

Key takeaway points

- We can help a traumatized person reboot their nervous systems using OMG (orient, move, ground) techniques.
- A key pastoral strategy is normalization: telling the person that what they are experiencing is entirely normal for what they have just been through.
- Another key pastoral strategy is connecting people to their resources (trauma responses cut us off from our resources).
- Most people will recover normal functioning in four to six weeks.
- NHS England advises *watchful waiting*, enabling people to recover through their natural coping mechanisms and systems of support.
- The first focus of immediate care is on basic needs: safety, water, food, shelter. Next comes psychological and emotional needs to feel valued and accepted. Listening is very important.
- The survivor is the expert.

Notes

1 National Health Service, 'Post-Traumatic Stress Disorder', *NHS*, www.nhs.uk/conditions/post-traumatic-stress-disorder-ptsd/treatment/, accessed 6.04.2020.

2 'Hearing to speech' is a phrase coined by Nelle Morton, 1985, *The Journey is Home*, Boston, MA: Beacon Press, pp. 202–10, 245n1. It describes the process of attention and listening that enables the speaker to discover and articulate what she or he is experiencing.

3 Jackson (2017, p. 26) is quoting Jamie Hacker Hughes.

4 For more information on what impacts human happiness and well-being around the world, see www.happinessresearchinstitute.com, accessed 27.11.2020.

5

Care That Heals

I have used the word *care* about 30 times thus far. Let's take a look at what it is and how it works.

In Old English, 'care' is about sorrow, anxiety and grief. The etymological development of the word began with 'cry' and moved through 'lamentation' to 'grief' and reflects the relational reality that we are pro-social creatures. When someone is distressed, we feel moved to respond in a caring way.

The mirror neurons in our brains may be at the heart of this natural response. In 1994, Italian scientists identified specialized cells in the cortex that fire in the brain as an individual watches the activity of another person, causing the observer's brain to mirror what is happening in the brain of the person who is acting (van der Kolk 2014, pp. 58–9). These cells, called mirror neurons, enable the development of language, among other things, and explain empathy and the caring response. When we see someone suffering, if we are awake and open to it, it is as though we are suffering ourselves and we want to respond. When we are overwhelmed, we are cut off from this response. Sometimes we intentionally turn off the response, as readily as we turn off the news when it becomes too much to bear.

Our mirror neurons enable our brains to mimic the brains of others and help our limbic systems to read other limbic systems. We pick up not only another person's activity but also their emotional state. Calm is infectious, as is anxiety; care too resounds in the nervous system.

Care is a key response to a traumatizing event. Our strategies in the acute and later phases after the terrible thing happens can be summarized by three C's: *Calm, Communication and Caring.*[1] All three elements help the traumatized nervous system to metabolize stress hormones and reboot. *Calm* derives from the fact that our calmness will be picked up and mimicked in the nervous systems around us. We strive to be less anxious as we pay attention to how we and others are impacted, normalize traumatic reactions and help people's nervous systems to reboot. *Communication* is about how people need clear, reliable information so that they know what to expect.[2] In Chapter 3 I stressed the importance of finding a source of reliable information. And *caring*, as I have said and will say again, is what we are made for: what enables us to develop, thrive, heal and flourish.

Care is most effective when it is *resonant*. Resonance happens when we sense that the person present to us 'gets' us, understands us and sees us with emotional warmth and generosity (Peyton 2017, p. xxiv). Reassurance (*everything will be all right*) is not resonance. When my daughter was 18 months old, she was hospitalized for a tracheal infection and experienced a complex febrile seizure. I was holding her, rocking back and forth as she was seizing and not breathing. I was chanting, 'Something is wrong, something is wrong.' The wise paediatrician looked me right in the eye and said, 'You're right. Something is wrong. We're going to do some tests.' I immediately began to calm down. She didn't assure me that all would be well; I would have intuitively known that that was not a given. (My daughter is fine 36 years on.)

Resonant care is warm and it is precise. It seeks to understand exactly what is going on for the person to whom we are present. It helps them to begin to connect their inner experience with the outer reality of what has happened. Resonant language includes wondering about and naming emotion, needs and physical sensations (Peyton 2017, p. xxv). When a person experiences resonant care, the alarmed limbic system further calms and begins to heal.

Neuroscience research has shown that human brains find their way back from distress to emotional balance in four main ways (Peyton 2017, p. 31):

1 The real or imagined presence of a person whom we feel cares about us (accompaniment)

2 Identifying what we are feeling (naming emotions – which I wrote about in Chapter 2)

3 Thinking about the situation in a different way (reframing)

4 Thinking about something else instead of what is troubling us (distraction)

When a person is traumatized, being accompanied by being cared for resonantly is more important than anything else. When someone is present to us, our amygdala (early warning centre) calms down, our stress hormone levels drop and we feel pain less (Peyton 2017, p. 35). The sense of overwhelm begins to abate. We begin to connect with ourselves.

When accompaniment is coupled with naming, with identifying what is happening inside (if it is safe to do so and the survivor is ready), forward movement is enabled. The agitated nervous system and body begin to relax. Named in the presence of warm acceptance – by ourselves or another – feelings can be worked with and lose their power to harm.

The third way that the brain finds its way back to balance – reframing – requires cognitive effort and is not possible by a hyper-aroused, traumatized brain. The fourth way – distraction – does not facilitate the integration of feeling and thinking that is the long-term goal of trauma recovery. However, it may provide moments of necessary respite. Accompaniment is our primary tool in the immediate aftermath of a traumatizing event, with naming a tool only if the survivor is ready for it.

The good news is that decent care in the immediate aftermath of a traumatizing event helps people to process the event and return to a new normal. They will be less likely to suffer distress over the long term.

Working with your 'window of welcome'

Offering resonant care can be a challenge. Each of us has a 'window of welcome' which is the amount and kind of emotional expression and intention that we can meet with warmth and understanding and respond to with resonance (Peyton

2017, p. 216). We may have a wide window of welcome for sorrow and a narrow one for anger or vice versa. Consider what feelings make you most uncomfortable. Those may be the ones for which you have a narrow window of welcome.

What happens when the person in front of us, or even we ourselves, express feelings that are not within the bounds of our window of welcome? We shift from operating out of the right hemisphere of our brain – the part of the brain that specializes in resonance, taking in and reading the body's emotional experience, and looking for the bigger picture – to operating out of the left hemisphere, which is oriented towards action and evaluation rather than understanding.[3] Both hemispheres are important and they are in constant interaction with each other. When the emotional temperature in the room starts to heat up as our window of welcome is exceeded, a shift to the left seeks to bring a cooling.

Shifts to the left, then, are attempts at self-protection, managing our own level of arousal. Examples of left shifts include when we minimize another's experience (*It's not that bad*), rationalize what has happened (*That must have happened because …*) or spiritualize it (*God wanted another angel in heaven*). Here are some indications that a left shift is being made:

- Failing to acknowledge the emotion that has been shown in words, gestures or facial expressions
- Offering a correction (*I'm sure the other person had a good intention*)
- Reframing the situation (*You can think of it this way …*)
- Attempting to fix the situation or give advice
- Micro-aggressions, e.g. generalizing a specific person into a group (*men always …*)
- Changing the subject

What do we do when, tuning into our felt sense, our discomfort starts to incline us to shift left? Notice it. Take a breath and maybe a break. Most importantly, be compassionate with yourself. Your window of welcome was formed by your life experience. Wonder about what you are feeling. Sarah Peyton's book *Your Resonant Self* has meditations and exercises to expand our capacities through healing our brains and establishing new neural pathways.

This leads me to reflect on the reality that when we are dealing with traumatizing events, there are always things we cannot see that are going on. We do not know what others are carrying that is impacting their response. And we do not know all that we ourselves carry. Pastoral counsellor and supervision trainer Ruth Layzell (2019, p. 202) calls these 'hidden narratives' and counsels us towards gentle and compassionate inquiry. Often it is an excessive reaction to something that provides a clue to invisible factors or that a previous trauma has been awakened. It is important not to judge such reactions harshly as a failure to cope. Rather, we notice the reactions with kindness. Life is hard; most of the time we are doing the best we can with what we've got.

More thoughts on care

While caring it is always important to remember that what works for one person may not work for another. We take our lead from the survivor, who is the expert in their trauma. Our role is to observe and listen carefully, hearing her or him into speech as they find their way. Our care is aimed at restoring agency as trauma leaves people feeling powerless. We respect that every survivor has potential resilience and natural healing processes. We connect people to their resources. We reclaim the ancient meaning of the word *comfort*: to strengthen.

And we make sure to care for the frontline carers. They need to be well-briefed, well led, and offered peer and social support (Williams, Bisson and Kemp 2014, p. 27). Acknowledging the value of what they are doing and alerting them to their own needs can prevent subsequent depression or other trauma responses. We watchfully wait and notice if people start to exhibit trauma symptoms, aware that these may be delayed or triggered and that first responders are at risk of secondary or vicarious trauma. More will be said about these phenomena in Chapter 7 (Superheroes).

Finally, when we encounter those who are in the small minority of people whose nervous systems get stuck in a trauma response – becoming hypervigilant or closing down – we are in over our heads. Most ministers do not have the requisite training in trauma recovery to help and the little we do know may end up causing harm. Trauma recovery is a long and painful journey (Herman 1992). Leave it to the experts. Our role is to continue to be a caring presence in practical, spiritual and emotionally supportive ways (Layzell 2019, p. 206).

Key takeaway points

- The Three C's – *calm, communication, care* – frame our responses to those who are traumatized.
- Care is most effective when it is resonant: warm and precise.
- Decent care in the immediate aftermath of a traumatizing event reduces distress in the long run.
- When our 'window of welcome' for emotion is exceeded, we tend to shift from our right (resonant, understanding) hemisphere to our left (evaluation, fix it). This is not resonant care.
- To comfort is to strengthen. People have potential resilience and natural healing processes.
- Care for the carers.
- Refer the small minority of survivors who have persistent, strong symptoms.

Notes

1 Thank you to Dr Kate Wiebe, Director of the Institute for Collective Trauma and Growth, for the framework of the three C's.

2 The key components of helpful communication post-trauma are honesty, clarity, brevity, and acknowledgement of gravity and uncertainty. Effective communication builds resilience and self-efficacy (Williams, Bisson and Kemp 2014, pp. 12–13, 17).

3 See Peyton (2017, pp. 63–6) for more on the right and left hemispheres.

6

A Special Case: Moral Injury

The previous chapters have described the brain-body response to a traumatizing event and how best to calm an agitated nervous system and enable the healing of normal post-traumatic stress. When the body gets stuck in those stress responses and there is lasting suffering, the individual may be suffering from Post-Traumatic Stress Disorder.[1] PTSD requires specialist mental health treatment; our role is to refer and to provide spiritual and emotional support.

In recent years, research has emerged identifying another type of trauma that results in similar symptoms to those of PTSD, one that the Church may have unique resources to offer to facilitate healing alongside professional help. First observed in returning veterans as combat trauma, I am talking about *moral injury*, a term first introduced in the 1990s (Shay 1994) and discussed in psychological research in 2009 (Litz et al. 2009).

There is no settled definition of moral injury at this point in time. It is not classified as a disorder, nor are there firm diagnostic markers. The foundation of the concept is rooted in human relationality and in the moral code that an individual develops that specifies the right and wrong ways to relate to other people. That moral code is integral to a person's identity (Boudreau 2020, p. 53). In Parts 2 and 3 you will read about assumptive frameworks and the narrative quality of identity.

Situations arise in life in which a person's moral code may be challenged or overcome by a complex confluence of psychological, environmental, cultural and organizational factors (Coady et al. 2020, p. 30). The situations studied in the original work on moral injury concerned veterans who were under the command of a trusted leader who acted immorally in a combat context, or who found themselves acting or failing to act in a combat situation in ways that contravened their moral code.[2] The system they were part of betrayed them into witnessing or committing what they felt to be deep wrongs. These betrayals and failures left lasting psychological, inter-personal, biological, spiritual and behavioural impacts on the veterans. This is moral injury: significant suffering that results from violations of a person's moral beliefs about themselves or the world, by what they did or didn't do, or by what they witnessed. It is a soul wound (Brock and Lettini 2012). Moral injury is not a disorder; it is evidence of moral consciousness. More than that, it can be a prophetic critique of societally accepted moral wrongs.

Moral injury may co-occur with PTSD[3] but it is not PTSD. It is shame- or guilt-based and rooted in values, rather than fear-based and rooted in having been violated or seriously threatened oneself (Lettini 2012, pp. 35–6; Moon 2020, p. 60). It may be manifested in anger, self-loathing, inability to trust, emotional dysregulation, hostility, despair – leading to social isolation, addiction, danger-seeking, self-harm or suicide (McDonald 2020, p. 8; Currier and McCormick 2020, p. 99).[4] The effect will be shaped by the severity of the wound and its impact on a person's identity. Zachary Moon (2020, p. 68), a practical theologian and former chaplain to veterans, says that 'Moral injury is best understood as a severe, debilitating moral anguish comparable to PTSD in seriousness and symptomology.'

Moral injury is at the extreme end of a spectrum of tested moral consciousness ranging from moral challenge through frustration to stress then distress and finally moral injury (Coady et al. 2020, p. 27). Its gravity can be such that an injured person may not be able to believe in a coherent moral framework.

It is increasingly being realized that military service may not be the only context for moral injury (Griffin et al. 2019, p. 356). And not all people who experience a potentially morally injurious situation are left with moral injury. Like all trauma responses, it is unique to the individual. Anyone whose work puts them in proximity of that which violates human life or dignity, who may be a witness or who has the responsibility or opportunity to act, could be at risk. Consider the firefighters whose standing orders instruct them to keep people within a burning tower block only for some of those people to perish, or the doctor who has to decide how to employ limited resources in the midst of overwhelming demand. Advocates for refugees and asylum seekers, prison officers and chaplains, human rights and disaster aid workers … the list goes on.

During the Covid pandemic it was recognized that NHS key workers were put in situations that were potentially morally injurious (Williamson, Murphy and Greenberg 2020). The potential risk factors for moral injury were identified as:

- If there is loss of life to a vulnerable person
- If leaders are perceived not to take responsibility for the event(s) and are unsupportive of staff
- If staff feel unaware of or unprepared for emotional and psychological consequences of decisions
- If the PMIE (potentially morally injurious event) occurs concurrently with exposure to other traumatic events (e.g. the death of a loved one)
- If there is a lack of social support following the PMIE (Williamson, Murphy and Greenberg 2020, p. 318)

The importance of the availability of timely psychological and social support for front-line workers was emphasized, as well as the awareness that moral injury is not amenable to the same treatments as PTSD. One of the challenges of moral injury is that shame and guilt impede people from seeking help. Three key preventative strategies were offered to limit moral injury in healthcare professionals during the pandemic: 1) enhanced decision-making support with complex decisions shared, 2) the provision of time and space for clinicians to 'decompress' and 3) staff working consistently within the same team (Roycroft et al. 2020, p. 312).

While not much has been written about it in the literature on moral injury, the Church and churches have a special vulnerability to inflicting it because of their role in society of providing a moral compass and a code. When the Church or its representatives betray the trust put in it, the damage can be severe. In recent decades, the scandal of clergy sexual abuse has been uncovered (Grosch-Miller 2019b, pp. 239–55). Such abuse causes primary trauma in the victims, trauma that often includes the devastation of spiritual grounding and the ability to trust. Clergy sexual abuse has been described as destroying the most sensitive parts of an individual's identity, their understanding of God as loving and the integrity of the institution (Pargament, Murray-Swank and Mahoney 2008, pp. 403–4). Alongside the primary victim who is traumatized and morally injured, a host of others involved directly or indirectly in the situation may suffer moral injury: the alleged or proven perpetrator, the families of victims and perpetrators, members of the congregation and Church officers. It is possible that the long length of time that it takes a congregation to recover from such a betrayal is in part because it is morally injured.

It is possible too that the Church's stance on homosexuality may result in moral injury in diverse ways. Although not written about in terms of moral injury, the deleterious impact of traditional Church teaching on lesbian, gay and bisexual people has been documented (Chalke, Sansbury and Streeter 2017). The impact includes a higher prevalence of suicide and suicidal ideation, thought to be one of the consequences in veterans who are morally injured. Gabriella Lettini (2020, pp. 37, 40–1) observes more generally that in the wider context of society, marginalized people living under systems of injustice that harm their sense of self, dignity and integrity may suffer moral injury.

On the other side of the homosexuality argument, people who have a strict moral code that disallows homosexual expression may be deeply challenged and disturbed by the Church's grappling with the issue. They may feel themselves marginalized and their integrity and that of the Church to be under attack.

Moral repair

The literature on moral repair focuses on the military context. There is some consensus about the road to repair: it is difficult and requires 'serious personal effort taken in the company of others' (McDonald 2020, p. 17). What has been damaged is one's identity in community. A witnessing community is the locus of healing (Larson 2020, p. 131).

The serious personal effort begins with disclosure. Thus a first step for the pastoral carer is compassionate, patient, non-judgemental listening – the kind of resonant care discussed in the previous chapter. The root of the suffering will be difficult to disclose. Listeners are cautioned not to make assumptions or to valorize the speaker or thank them for their military service. To rush in seeking to ameliorate pain by saying 'it wasn't your fault' shames the shamed and impedes what needs to happen (Moon 2020, p. 65; Ramsay 2020, p. 118). Space must be made for soul-searching and truth-telling so that the speaker has the chance to integrate their malfeasance or what they saw into an understanding of the self as imperfect but acceptable and worthy of love (McDonald 2020, p. 10). To do that, it must be disclosed.

You will recall from Chapter 4 that not everyone who is traumatized needs to talk about what happened, and that there is the possibility of re-traumatization if the person is not ready to speak of it and is encouraged to do so. Here we see the importance of assessing what is really going on. It is difficult to distinguish between moral injury and PTSD and a person may be suffering from both. A pastoral carer must tread lightly, refer when symptoms are severe and follow the person's lead when it comes to accompanying the journey of moral repair.

It is also important to acknowledge how difficult it may be to hear the story. Shelly Rambo (2017, pp. 109–43) describes the healing work of Warriors Journey Home (WJH), a veterans' group in Ohio.[5] The name given to the civilian members who support the veterans' healing journey is that of 'Strongheart'. One of their primary roles is to listen to the war stories; it is an act of courage to listen and to withhold judgement (Rambo 2017, pp. 117–18).

The serious personal work to be done by one who has been morally injured may include examining beliefs – about themselves, others or God – that have not served them well (Litz et al. 2009, p. 703). In further chapters we will look at how trauma can be de-illusioning and that making sense of what happened may include rebuilding or reframing one's assumptions. Moral repair also requires being able to accept and forgive oneself. Early psychological research indicated that 'dialogue with a caring and benevolent moral authority' can be helpful (Litz et al. 2009, pp. 703–4). This could be God or a person. Here too we see the power of community witness that the Church may be well placed to offer: *If this community forgives me, maybe I can forgive myself. If they love me, maybe I'm lovable* (Larson 2020, p. 125). Part of accepting forgiveness is the making of amends or reparation – an active choosing to do good. The exercise of agency buttresses a reclaimed moral goodness and reconnection with a moral value system. Research concludes the list of reparative strategies with fostering reconnection with significant others and identifying values and goals for the future (Litz et al. 2009, p. 704).

The role of a healing community is to listen and hold difficult truths, and to seek to understand, to witness to healing, and to reintegrate the person who has been morally injured. It may also be willing to accept a shared responsibility for that injury (Griffin et al. 2019, p. 357), if for instance it has uncritically supported unjust wars or unwittingly created an environment that enabled abuse. Rambo (2017, p. 124) writes of the work of healing she witnessed in WJH as a collective process of soul development, not only for those who are morally injured but for those who come alongside, the Stronghearts.

Spiritual resources and the Christian community

Moral repair is not a one-off experience but a lifelong process. Given that faith is a source of morality, it is no surprise that the Christian community has particular practices and resources that contribute to the work. Among those are ritual expressions of forgiveness and reconciliation, the nourishment of Word and sacrament, the cultivation of nourishing spiritual disciplines, and the encouragement to faithfulness and vocation. In Part 2 you will read about the power of lamentation (Chapter 10) and more generally the treasure trove that is the Bible (Chapter 11). Lament is one of two particularly helpful resources that have been identified in spiritual care for those who have been morally injured. The other is the notion prominent in the Bible that God pursues those in need of forgiveness to offer hope for a new future (Ramsay 2020, p. 115).

Biblical stories that may have particular resonance for people suffering from moral injury include Jacob wrestling at the Jabbok and the Gerasene demoniac. In Genesis chapter 32, verses 22–32, Jacob sends his wives, children, servants and live-stock to ford the Jabbok and remains alone. There he wrestles a stranger (God, an angel, his conscience?) all night long in preparation for his first encounter with his brother Esau after many years. He is confronting the deception he undertook to engineer wrangling the firstborn blessing that should have gone to Esau. He wrestles and wrestles and declares he will not let go until he receives a blessing. The stranger blesses him and gives him a new name, Israel, one who struggles or strives with or for God. They release their hold on each other and he limps off, bearing the mark of the struggle. The work of moral repair makes its mark; those who engage it are not restored to lost innocence but renewed with deepened wisdom about the human condition. Imagine using a practice such as *lectio divina* with this story: naming the wrestling, the blessing, the limp (Ramsay 2020, p. 119).

The Gerasene demoniac (Mark 5) too can be read as a morally injured person. Michael Yandell (2020, pp. 72–7), a veteran himself, conceives of the demoniac as a former member of a Roman legion: he had left the legion but the legion would not leave him. His identity is disrupted and conflated by his war experience; he is left among the tombs, howling and bruis-ing himself. He recognizes Jesus and begs him not to torment him, seeing Jesus as both a potential source of redemption but also of condemnation. When healed, he begs Jesus to take him with him. But Jesus refuses and gives him work to do. He is left to deliver the good news to his community – who must then reckon with him and who they are in relation to him, to recognize his humanity just as he is to recognize theirs.

The restoration of humanity is the work of moral repair: the humanity of the sufferer and the humanity of those whose suffering he or she may have witnessed, caused or failed to address. Recognizing the humanity of others brings us back to our own (Cotrill 2020, p. 157).

Key takeaway points

- Moral injury may occur when an individual acts, fails to act or witnesses such actions or failures by a trusted leader in ways that violate his or her moral code.
- A person who is morally injured may also be traumatized. It is difficult to distinguish between moral injury and Post-Traumatic Stress Disorder as the symptoms are similar.
- The result of a moral injury can be self-loathing, anger, despair, emotional dysregulation, an inability to trust or to believe in a coherent moral framework, with outcomes of social isolation, addiction, high-risk activity, self-harm or suicide.
- Moral repair is a difficult journey requiring serious personal effort and a supportive community, and entailing full disclosure, acceptance and forgiveness, reconnection with significant others, and a reclaiming of values and goals for the future.

Notes

1 See Chapter 1 above, note 2, regarding PTSD.

2 In the psychological literature there is a distinction between those morally injured by witnessing betrayal by a trusted leader (betrayal model of moral injury, based on Shay's work) and that suffered by persons who perpetrated against their moral code (perpetrator model). See McDonald (2020, pp. 8–12) and Griffin et al. (2019, pp. 355–6).

3 A person suffering from moral injury may be traumatized and experience PTSD symptoms or may be vicariously or secondarily traumatized from working with or being exposed to traumatized people. The risk of the latter types of traumatization is discussed in the next chapter. It can be difficult to distinguish moral injury from PTSD.

4 It is thought that moral injury contributes to 22 veteran suicides a day in the USA (Ramsay 2020, p. 113).

5 See also Larson (2020, pp. 123–33) for a description of some effective faith-based community models of caring for the morally injured. Note that one group leader came to believe that their program was not replicable in other places, requiring a level of spiritual generosity and maturity that not all congregations have (p. 125).

7

Superheroes (Self-care is not an Optional Extra)

Self-care is an essential habit of the heart in ministry. The Three C's of calm, communication and care are habits of the heart for a congregation that, practised in ordinary time, build resilience and in times of crisis help people on the journey of recovery. So it is with self-care. Making it a habit of the heart in ordinary time will stand you in particularly good stead when the terrible thing happens.

I call these habits of the heart in an attempt to emphasize that we do them out of love more than duty. Perhaps some find duty – the 'shoulds' – compelling and effective. But for me, and I suspect for many, attending to the daily discipline of caring for body, mind and soul as an act of love is more motivating than adding it to the 'to-do' list.

Witnessing and accompanying the pain of others can impact us, sometimes strongly. It may resonate with our own life experience, triggering responses that surprise us. Or we may experience vicarious or secondary trauma, equally surprising and distressing.

As will become clear in Part 2 on collective trauma, leading a congregation in the aftermath of a traumatizing event will require our attention for a long time: possibly two to five years for a clear-cut event and longer for more complex or unfolding traumas. We will be in it for the long haul. Self-care is not an optional extra.

This quote is from a book I have been reading and re-reading for almost 20 years, Parker Palmer's slim gem *Let Your Life Speak* (2000, pp. 30–1):

Self-care is never a selfish act – it is simply good stewardship of the only gift I have, the gift I was put on earth to offer others. Anytime we can listen to true self and give the care it requires, we do it not only for ourselves, but for the many others whose lives we touch.

Particularly when the terrible thing happens but also throughout the long post-trauma journey, care for ourselves can be very difficult. We may be traumatized and cut off from our resources. And even if we are not, surrounded by the suffering of others it is difficult to act in our own interest. Yet self-care is one of the most important things that will enable us to do what we need to do – to be calm, caring and wise in discernment possibly over a very long period of time. Recall the instruction you hear at the beginning of a flight: 'Put on your own oxygen mask before helping others'. Cultivating a habit of self-care now not only will make it easier for you to access your resources and respond in a crisis, but it will build your resilience and enhance your ministry day by day.

A large part of self-care is self-awareness. Our bodies are giving us useful and important information all the time. Recall the information flow from the enteric brain up to the head brain which we encountered in Chapter 2. Yet often we may have a hard time hearing what the body is telling us, especially if we spend a lot of time at a desk or have learned to ignore our bodies to survive or to achieve.

We disregard our bodies at our peril. When we exceed our limits, we will eventually experience the consequences – illness, burnout or general misery. Tuning into our felt sense (recall Chapter 2) helps us to keep appropriate boundaries in our pastoral caring and to discern between courses of action in our leadership. It will help us to know when we need to stop and rest or re-create so that we will be able to give our best in God's service. As I explored in Chapter 5 on Care, being aware of our window of welcome helps us to care resonantly for others as well as ourselves. Noticing our own surprising responses with warmth and curiosity will help us to work with the hidden and not so hidden stuff we all bring to our work.

Being in our bodies takes practice. It is an element of a habit of self-care and an essential part of post-traumatic recovery. Bessel van de Kolk, author of *The Body Keeps the Score*, emphasizes learning to meet the body and listen to it in his work with trauma victims. He encourages practices like yoga, tai chi and other movement-based activities to connect people to their bodies.

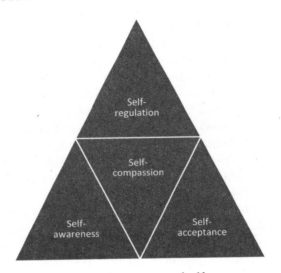

Figure 6: Components of self-care

Self-care encompasses self-awareness, self-acceptance, self-compassion and self-regulation. Self-acceptance draws down the barriers of defence that get in the way of working with who we are and what we have. Self-compassion enables us to receive information, from within or from others, without defensiveness and to respond to our very human foibles and failures with kindness. We know through our pastoral practice that when people are met with judgement or defensiveness, they throw up barriers to protect themselves. We do the same. We can't grow when we are well-defended. Nor can we learn when we feel shamed. We also can't lead well. To lead, to learn and to live well, we must be willing to experience and acknowledge our vulnerability (Brown 2018b).

Self-compassion is rooted in self-love, the healthy kind of love that is assumed in the great commandment to love God and our neighbour as ourselves (Matthew 22.36–39). When we have enough love or compassion for ourselves, we know that we are worth taking care of, worth dressing and addressing our wounds, worth doing whatever it is that we need to do to steward ourselves. When we don't, the well of love dries up and we have little or nothing to give.

The self-regulation aspect of self-care is how we manage and resource ourselves. Being aware of who and how we really are enables us to manage ourselves, stepping back so that we can think through things and respond thoughtfully rather than reactively. When I am feeling stressed and anxious and know that my bandwidth for challenge is small, I can remove myself from situations that will test that bandwidth. I remember the week that we were without heat or hot water and the internet was not working well. At one point I found myself shouting, 'I can't work like this!' (Note that the pandemic was going on, our region was experiencing alarming rises in infection rates and Brexit was around the corner. The thrum of anxiety was heightening everywhere.) The telephone engineer came and took a few hours to fix external faults, after which he turned to me and started to say, 'There are more problems I can't fix …' As I felt the heat rise up my neck, I looked up at my partner and said, 'I can't handle any more. I'm going to leave the room and let you deal with this.' Fortunately, David could do that.

Resourcing ourselves is an exercise in listening to the wholeness of our being. Another word for self-regulation is self-discipline, a word with the same root as 'disciple'. Both words derive from the Latin *disciplina*, meaning knowledge or instruction. Paying attention, listening and learning, we grow in our capacity to regulate and care for ourselves – physically (rest, exercise, nutrition); emotionally (friendship, working with our feelings, art, music, play); and spiritually (our connection to God, the earth, the faith community and ourselves). Self-compassion is at the heart of resilience and self-regulation is its muscle.

Self-care in the aftermath of trauma

In the next chapter you will learn that there are phases of a collective trauma, the first of which is the heroic phase. Heroism is, in part, a physiological response. You will recall that when the amygdala sounds the alarm and the hypothalamus starts releasing stress hormones, we are catapulted into fight, flight or freeze. Both flight and fight responses are powerful physical reactions that propel movement. People may do heroic things when the situation calls for it, and as they do agency hormones are released that metabolize stress hormones.

In a collective trauma the heroic phase sees an outpouring of resources aimed at addressing the crisis. It is an inspiring time – 'Exhilarating!', as the minister said when the microphone was pushed into his face. Churches may get filled with donations of water, blankets, clothing, refrigerators, all sorts depending on the crisis. The logistics of organizing the response is all-consuming. You and your volunteers will be tempted to work countless hours and not count the cost, to be superheroes. Running on adrenaline you may feel terrific, even high.

Dr Sarah Horsman, Warden of the Society of Mary and Martha at Sheldon which supports people in Christian ministry,[1] advises that the feeling of being on a high is a warning sign (Southgate 2019a, pp. 261–2). We are finite beings. She describes a human function curve:[2] the amount of effort you are putting in against the amount of performance you are getting out.

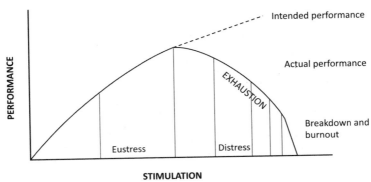

Figure 7: Human function curve

After we reach the top of that curve things will begin to decline in our physical health or behaviour as we run on overdraft energy. The danger of the high is that we become overconfident and that we fail to count the cost of running on overdraft energy. We will have to pay for it at some point. These are biological realities.

Horsman also observes that many of the people who come to Sheldon for recovery after leading a congregation through a tragedy will say 'I was already over-stretched and then this came along' (Southgate 2019a, p. 260). She makes a strong argument for not living in permanent overstretch. In other words, she makes a strong argument for a habit of self-care. The Revd Dr Harriet Harris, University Chaplain of the University of Edinburgh, says that we need to replenish ourselves three times more than we think we do (Harris 2020).

Vicarious and secondary trauma

Clergy and first responders to a crisis are susceptible to delayed trauma reactions and to becoming vicariously or secondarily traumatized. Adequate self-care may prevent this kind of second-tier traumatization. Self-awareness will help us to respond and to recover if we find ourselves in that situation.

What are vicarious trauma and secondary trauma? There is no settled distinction at this point in time between the two. Both result in the clergy person or first responder experiencing some kind of trauma response without having been primarily traumatized. One way to distinguish between them is by the cause and the symptoms. Vicarious trauma may result from the drip, drip, drip of accumulated exposure to other people's trauma and the symptoms may be diverse. In contrast, secondary trauma may be when you start experiencing a specific symptom of a particular person for whom you are caring or to whom you are close.[3] The symptoms of either can be those of Post-Traumatic Stress Disorder.

This is a list of signs to watch out for in yourself:

- Feeling helpless and hopeless
- A sense that one can never do enough
- Hypervigilance
- Diminished creativity
- Inability to embrace complexity
- Minimizing (denial, dismissal)
- Chronic exhaustion
- Physical ailments
- Inability to listen/deliberate avoidance
- Sense of persecution
- Dissociative moments
- Guilt
- Fear
- Anger and cynicism
- Inability to empathize/numbing
- Grandiosity: an inflated sense of the importance of one's work
- Addictions

A note about addiction: in the field of traumatology, addiction is considered to be a coping mechanism (Peyton 2017, pp. xxxii, 33).

If you are experiencing some of the listed signs, have a good look at what is going on inside and around you, increase your self-care activities and find someone to talk to – a supervisor, counsellor, spiritual director or physician.

Remember: there is no shame in being traumatized. It is beyond our control and that goes for being vicariously or secondarily traumatized as well as primarily traumatized. Our body is trying to save us. The wise response is to listen to what it is telling us, what we know deep down, and to get some support.

Horsman offers a 'canary in a coalmine' exercise, asking, 'What are your personal and particular symptoms that are warning signs for you that you're not 100% okay?' (Southgate 2019a, p. 270).[4] She advises that the more specific the answer, the better. For one person it might be that they have not had a homecooked meal in a week. For another it may be that they haven't read a non-work related book in the past month or taken any exercise all week. As a comfort eater I know that if I snack indeterminately at night, something is weighing on me (and it will weigh elsewhere the next morning). You will know the clues for you.

In our teaching of ordinands and clergy, we ask them to reflect on these questions:

- How do you schedule 'off duty' time in your diary? How do you feel doing that?
- What are your resources? Name the practices or activities that
  - keep you connected to God, yourself and others
  - give you resilience and strength
  - keep you healthy physically and emotionally
- What are six caring relationships that can sustain you?
- What is your 'canary in a coalmine'?

We ask them, after they have completed the reflection, to share the information with someone who can remind them of their resources when they most need them. You will recall that trauma cuts us off from our resources. We need reminding when we are caught up in our own or someone else's trauma.

I offer the wisdom of the Salvation Army's Well Being Unit.[5] They remind us that there are many things we can do to take care of ourselves:

Spiritually: Enjoy the moment, feed the soul (inner being), self-reflection, listen to music, participate in a spiritual community, visit a special place, prayer and other spiritual exercises.

Psychologically: Self-awareness, self-reflection, journaling, learning, focus on breathing, exercise, sleep, join interest or support groups, give thanks for three good things.

Emotionally: Exercise compassion, laugh, family time, talk, eat, enjoy the moment, practise forgiveness.

Physically: Eat; breathe; exercise – walk, garden, cycle, gym, park run; sport; visit art galleries, etc.; sleep.

Finally, a book that is particularly relevant to surviving and thriving during difficult times is Justine Allain-Chapman's *Resilient Pastors: The Role of Adversity in Healing and Growth* (2012). Allain-Chapman describes the journey from adversity to altruism drawing on the literature of resilience, scripture, the desert fathers and mothers, and the writings of Rowan Williams, developing the notion of ministers as wounded healers. The three elements that enable the journey are: facing into the struggle (which may require retreating to a place of safety), engaging the self and relying on positive relationships.

Self-sacrifice?

The emphasis on self-care in this chapter is not meant to undermine the reality that there may be times when we are called to suffer or to sacrifice. Prayerful discernment of such a call is a serious matter. If it is a true call, it will be accompanied by the sense of consolation spoken of in Ignatian spirituality. The material in this chapter is intended to equip us to resist pressures to take up other people's crosses or to overextend and thus compromise our ability to fulfil our own vocations.

Observations about self-care during an unfolding complex trauma

When there is a collective trauma that is unfolding and unpredictable, self-care is even more necessary and perhaps even more difficult than when the trauma is a single event. Human brains like safety and predictability and will be working overtime trying to process changing events. People are likely to have a thrum of anxiety in the background that they may not be aware of unless they are paying attention to their comfort-seeking behaviours. They may be exhausted and irritable. Given that death and joblessness are happening to others, the silent symptoms may go unnoticed and unremarked. But the body is keeping the score. Focusing on the basics of adequate nutrition, rest, exercise and some kind of social contact are essential. So too is gentle acceptance, day by day, hour by hour, of what is happening in one's body and brain. Be present and kind; accept unpredictable feelings; lower the goalposts of achievement.

As the Covid pandemic rolled on unpredictably, people began to exhibit the symptoms of chronic stress. It became all the more important to exercise. Even low-intensity movement counteracts stress-induced inflammation in the body and increases neural connections in the brain. Other stress-management strategies include engaging in spiritual practices, including meditation and mindfulness which can lead to positive, structural and functional changes in the brain. Staying in close contact with friends and family, even staring into a pet's eyes, may counteract inflammation. And learning something new flexes our brain's capacity to grow and change (Pattani 2020). Dr Luanna Marques (2020), an anxiety specialist, recommends: limiting exposure to daily news to once a day, anchoring yourself in the present, and creating a structure to manage uncertainty that includes clear work-life boundaries, regular breaks and connection with others.

For those who moved to leading worship online when church buildings were closed, additional stressors emerged. Without the natural feedback loop of embodied interaction during or after the service, worship leaders were deprived of being able to sense the shared meaningfulness of what they were doing. Ministers are human beings, with all the needs and wants that come with embodied being. There is no shame in that. Noticing the impact of events and sharing thoughts and feelings with colleagues helped in managing the vicissitudes of pandemic living.

The next chapters will discuss further what happens when a group or community is traumatized, and the resources at our disposal to help to manage the distress and dislocation.

Key takeaway points

- Self-care is a habit of the heart which will build resilience and help you respond to tragic events.
- In times of crisis self-care is not an optional extra.
- Components of self-care include self-awareness, self-acceptance, self-compassion and self-regulation.
- Clergy and first responders are susceptible to delayed trauma reactions as well as to vicarious or secondary trauma.
- We need to replenish ourselves three times more than we think.
- Name your self-care resources and strategies and share them with someone who will remind you when you most need it.

Notes

1 See Sheldon, www.sheldon.uk.com/, accessed 29.04.2020. Note that the Sheldon Community runs the Sheldon Hub, an online community supporting people in ministry: www.sheldonhub.org/, accessed 29.04.2020.

2 This is known as the Yerkes-Dodson Law, originally developed by psychologists Robert M. Yerkes and John Dillingham Dodson in 1908. Figure 7 is derived from the National Health Service, Scotland Deanery, www.scotlanddeanery.nhs.scot/trainee-information/thriving-in-medicine/resilience-stress-and-a-growth-mindset/, accessed 8.12.2020. The original is attributed to Dr Peter Nixon.

3 Rothschild (2006, pp. 12–15) notes that the terms 'burnout', 'secondary traumatization', 'vicarious traumatization' and 'compassion fatigue' are used interchangeably in therapist literature. She offers these distinctions: compassion fatigue can apply to any suffering as a result of helping others; burnout is an extreme experience of compassion fatigue manifested in health problems or a negative outlook on life; secondary traumatization happens to people close to a primarily traumatized person (e.g. family) or who were an eyewitness; and vicarious traumatization comes from less direct exposure to the trauma of others.

4 See also Layzell (2019, pp. 206–7) on the need for self-care and support and Kraus, Holyan and Wismer (2017, pp. 64–7) who recommend that clergy create daily, weekly and monthly self-care plans.

5 Thank you to Major Maureen Doncaster of the UK Salvation Army, who shared her 'Tips for maintaining well being and building resilience'.

PART 2

Collective Trauma

Part 1 focused primarily on the impact of a traumatizing event on the individual. Now we turn to collective trauma. When may a group, community or nation be said to be traumatized?

8

The Hurting Whole

The study of collective trauma is more recent than that of individual trauma, with research primarily evaluating the impact on communities of one-off events such as floods, fires, earthquakes and terror attacks. As multifaceted global phenomena such as pandemics, economic dislocation and the climate crises batter the world, our understanding of collective trauma will grow.

It is currently thought that collective trauma may arise in one of two ways (Veerman and Ganzevoort 2001). The first is when a group or community contains a significant number of traumatized individuals or significant members of a community are traumatized. In this case the pain of individuals radiates outwards and impacts the functioning of the larger community. Consider, for example, the accidental death of several young people and key staff on a school field trip in a road traffic accident. In this kind of collective trauma, the individual trauma of fellow students, staff and family members may cause collective trauma.

The second way it may arise is if there is an event or series of events that impacts some individuals directly but that also impacts the structure (ways of relating) and the assumptive framework of the group in ways that threaten the lives of some individuals. In this kind of collective trauma normal elements of individual trauma – powerlessness and helplessness, acute disruption of normal existence and extreme discomfort – apply to the whole group. Examples of this kind of collective trauma include the devastation of communities by war, forced relocation, corporate or government malfeasance (e.g. the Aberfan mining spoil tip collapse in Wales and the Buffalo Creek slurry flood in West Virginia), fire, flood and other natural disasters.

The Covid-19 pandemic, which saw entire nations on lock-down as the disease progressed around the world, arguably was also this kind of collective trauma. In the pandemic people's normal ways of living and relating to one another were altered radically. The pandemic affected individuals through disease and death and the economic impact of restrictions; it shattered assumptions of invulnerability and control.

A collective trauma is compounded when a community's or a government's response to the original traumatizing event or events causes further individual or collective trauma. In the case of the pandemic, failures to provide adequate personal protection equipment (PPE) for health, social care, transport and other key workers resulted in loss of life among them. Government-imposed lockdowns and restrictions resulted in lost income, job losses and failed businesses. The unfolding trauma of the pandemic left devastated families in its wake and impacted the physical and mental health of significant parts of the population.

A third type of collective trauma has been suggested: cultural trauma. Cultural trauma is when a horrendous event so impacts a group that their future identity is changed in fundamental and irrevocable ways (Alexander 2004, p. 1). An example of cultural trauma is posited to have resulted from the enslavement of African peoples in the fifteenth–nineteenth centuries and the mid-twentieth-century Holocaust.

Life together

We considered the pro-social nature of the human being, our need for relationship and connection, in Part 1. In Part 2 we look a little more closely at what enables us to meet our needs and to function in the world, and how that is impacted by a traumatizing event or series of events.

Psychologist Ronnie Janoff-Bulman (1992) theorizes that human life is structured by fundamental assumptions about the world and about the self that enable us to make sense of the world and function in it. The three basic assumptions are that 1) the world is benevolent, 2) the world is meaningful – it is ordered and comprehensible, and 3) the self is worthy.[1] These preconscious ways of understanding the world and the self are formed in infancy, childhood and adolescence through the child's experience of a good enough primary carer. They provide a strongly held frame of reference that enables us to trust that we can recognize what is happening, plan and act. In other words, they provide us with enough safety, stability and coherence to relate to others and the world in ways that work.

These fundamental assumptions provide an ultimately illusory sense of invulnerability and of control. We tend to cling to these assumptions because we need them to feel safe and secure enough to function and to make sense of the world and our lives. They are remarkably resistant to change, even in the face of contradictory evidence. A traumatizing event rips the veil from our eyes and shatters some or all of these assumptions, provoking an intense psychological crisis as we are confronted with our vulnerability and our mortality. The crisis is only resolved when we as individuals or a community are able to adapt or create a set of fundamental assumptions that are positive enough to permit stability and coherence while taking into account that terrible things can happen. This is something that happens over a long time. How it happens will be explored in Part 3.

The shattering of assumptions is a hallmark of both individual and collective trauma. The journey towards reconstruction can be described as one that takes place over time and entails movement through recognizable phases. Although the description of the phases below is set out to look like a straightforward trek to a new normal, it is not. There may be circling back and revisiting; the experience often may feel chaotic. The phases describe a general direction or mood and help us to understand the characteristics and needs of different times in the life of a community moving towards recovery.

Phases of collective trauma response

Trauma specialist Dr Claude Chemtob describes the journey of post-traumatic recovery as beginning with 'United We Stand' as the community rallies and pulls together in the immediate aftermath of a traumatizing event. This is followed by a period of 'Molasses and Minefields' as people tire, stressors accumulate, offence is easily taken and the once united community begins to fragment into smaller groups for safety. The final stage of 'Recovery' happens as the community creates a positive vision of the new normal (Saul 2014, pp. 77–8).

The Institute of Collective Trauma and Growth (ICTG, www.ictg.org) devised a Phases of Collective Trauma Response chart that gives a visual representation of the post-trauma recovery journey. Available as a resource on their website and reproduced as Appendix C, it is derived in part from US government agency studies of what communities experienced after being hit by natural disasters.[2] The chart is heuristic, not prescriptive. No community's journey will look exactly like another's; trauma and recovery are shaped by the severity and nature of the event and its consequences, and the culture and context of the community. Nonetheless the chart provides a general sense of direction and a conversation tool for those seeking to understand what the journey ahead may be like. Here it is:

The Y-axis charts emotions (low to high) and the X-axis plots time. The ICTG observes that this journey can take two to five years or longer. In cases of clergy sexual abuse it may take as long as ten years (Grosch-Miller 2019b, p. 248). A congregation may carry behavioural marks of that betrayal for much longer.

Of special note are the kinds of collective trauma that go on for a long time and evolve, like the Grenfell Tower fire in 2017 and the Covid-19 pandemic. When the traumatizing event keeps morphing and adding layer upon layer of trauma, the journey becomes more complex and harder to grasp. People and communities will be in different phases and new events cause new trauma responses, fatiguing an already stretched

Figure 8: ICTG Phases of Collective Trauma Response

system. The chaos and unpredictability may make it difficult to generalize or for a direction of travel to coalesce. Leaders pay attention and try to catch the direction of the wind while improvising and employing strategies that seem to resonate. The information below and in the rest of the book can resource that kind of creative thinking. Indeed, as will be observed below, creativity and improvisation help communities live into a new normal in every collective trauma. Note however that our brains and energy levels may not be able to sustain creative improvisation until some time has passed. Survival is the name of the game in the early phases. Survival and adaptation.

Looking closely at the ICTG chart, note the horizontal line in the upper left-hand corner. This represents where the community was before the precipitating event. The terrible thing happens with an impact like a punch to the gut and people quickly rise to the occasion to respond, often heroically. The *heroic phase* is the fight/flight response in full flow, powering acts of bravery, kindness and generosity. Recall what is going on in the brain-body during trauma: the burst of activity is helping to calm the nervous system as agency hormones are released and stress hormones metabolized.

This phase can last days, weeks, months or even over a year.[3] At the beginning it may be dominated by the practicalities of meeting basic needs: getting people out of harm's way, search and rescue, clean up, providing mental health first aid. The Trauma Response Toolkit (Chapter 3) can help you to organize an effective first response. One of the challenges of leadership in this phase is to channel the heroic energy and also to be thinking about how to sustain and support people who are on the front line.

The heroic phase is powerful, seductive and exhilarating. Humanity never looked so good; we were made for this! United we stand! The community is suddenly cohesive and coherent. The feel-good factor of this phase is such that it is difficult for people to let go of it. They resist the downward spiral that inevitably follows. But that level of energy and cohering good will is not sustainable over the long haul. Recall the human function chart introduced in Chapter 7 on self-care and the dangers of the feeling of being on a high. Nor is the burst of communal cohesion sustainable, based as it is on temporary emotional ties and a shallow cognitive base. It reflects individuals' need to respond, the social mood and the communal need for order in the midst of chaos (Veerman and Ganzevoort 2001, pp. 7–8). It will deteriorate.

The *disillusionment phase* begins as the wear and tear of heroism takes its toll and cracks begin to appear in the unified front. It may be difficult to discern when you are moving into this phase. Perhaps Dr Chemtob's description of 'Molasses and Minefields' helps. This is a phase that includes exhaustion, low energy, tensions in the community that may become outright conflicts, hopelessness and the utter unpredictability of emotional responses in you and in others. Clergy are most in need of supervision or consultancy in this phase but least likely to seek it out. Our biochemistry works against us: we feel bad and are not inclined to seek help.[4]

In the disillusionment phase not everyone needs the same thing or responds in the same way. Recall the uniqueness of individual traumatized experiences. Some may metabolize the trauma relatively quickly and are ready to move on; others may not. In short it is a messy, chaotic, difficult phase. There is no way to come out on the other side except to walk through it, step by plodding step. This phase generally lasts for weeks or many months depending on the severity and particulars of the trauma.

Important things are happening in the disillusionment phase. People are resting and recovering from the initial shock and heroism of the first phase. There is a settling into the facts of what happened, or is happening, and its impacts. Energy is focused on survival and adaptation. In an unfolding, unpredictable situation, people are looking for ground firm enough to stand on and becoming able to hold opposite ideas in their minds (we will do X next month; we may not be able to do X next month). They also are learning to cope with chronic stress. Losses are being named and grieved. At the same time new possibilities and initiatives may be sparking energy among some. It is a complex phase and all the energies emerging play some function in the journey of recovery.

Note the lumpiness of the line as it follows its trajectory downward in the ICTG chart. There may be short bursts of energy where everything does not seem so awful. Note too that the downward trend slowly flattens out, eventually beginning to turn upwards. As the chart says, you know that the disillusionment phase has ended when most people accept the grievous loss that no heroics can fix and begin to be able to hold the thought that life is not all bad, good things exist too. *You cannot force this or make it happen.* People need a rest and recoupment period, and they need time to begin to make sense of what has happened. People also need a sense of safety – which may be in short supply in unfolding crises like pandemics. Just as decent care in the aftermath of a traumatizing event reduces the distress and long-term suffering of victims, so too good enough leadership through the disillusionment phase will enable people to move towards hope. Do not stress about whether your leadership will be good enough. Put one foot in front of the other and do what you can. Pastoral and liturgical strategies for this phase and the next are set out in Chapters 9–12.

The *rebuilding and restoration phase* is characterized by a general sense of moving forward. Sometimes this is a two-steps-forward, three-steps-back kind of experience. The line is even lumpier in this phase, with surges and fallbacks. The downs happen when traumatic memory is triggered (for example, by a similar event in the news or an anniversary) or conflict breaks out. Alongside continued grieving and memorial activity there also will be new ideas and initiatives and the energy to make things happen. The community is living into a new way, integrating the experience of the traumatizing event into its story.

The final phase is called *wiser living*. The line has evened out. The grief of what has happened has been individually and collectively lived with and lamented, the struggle has been integrated and is no longer avoided, and the faithful remnant has found a new normal. You will notice that the line is a little lower on the page than where the community started. We are changed by trauma, awakened to our vulnerability, aware that terrible things can happen – and that we can live through them. Innocence has been lost; the community's wisdom has deepened. People are able to hold the complex and tragic nature of human life with greater grace and resilience. Both life and faith are grounded in reality.

Recovery from collective trauma

You will recall that early on the traumatized brain functions as though the emotional brain has hijacked the cognitive brain. In collective trauma the job of the leader is to serve as the prefrontal cortex – thinking, planning, evaluating, imagining possibilities – in relation to the emotional brain, bringing as whole a brain as possible to the situation. If the leader is traumatized this can be difficult. Consultative processes bring more brain power and perspective into the room as the community travels through the long journey that is post-trauma recovery.

Jack Saul, a psychologist who directs the International Trauma Studies Program in New York City, argues persuasively (2014) that collective trauma calls for a collective response. While a minister and their team will have an eye on responding to traumatized individuals, they also will need regularly to step back to look at the whole and ask what will be most helpful to the larger group. The chapters that follow this one will look more specifically at strategies aimed at helping the congregation recover. The following paragraphs provide some information and overarching principles behind collective recovery.

Every community impacted by a traumatizing event will recover in its own way, which will be shaped by its internal narrative,[5] its history and culture, its resources, and the circumstances. Saul (2014, p. 103) observes that communities 'have the capacity to heal themselves and that the greatest resources for recovery are the community members themselves'. Just as the survivor is the expert in an individual trauma and it is the pastoral carer's job to connect people to their resources, one of the important roles of a community leadership team is to call forth and connect the community to its resources, restoring agency and respecting the power and responsibility of the community. Saul advocates a Community Resilience Model of trauma recovery, working with and supporting a community's natural links and resources. This model harnesses collective processes of adaptation and mobilization of capacities to strengthen the community-building blocks of families, systems, networks and individuals. Recovery is primarily relational, based on keyworkers seeking to rebuild the trusting and caring relationships that are foundational to a group.

There are four themes Saul identifies as characteristic of community resilience and recovery work (Saul 2014, pp. 105–6):

1 Building community and enhancing social connectedness (the 'matrix of healing');
2 Collectively telling the story of the community's experience and response, including the widest diversity of voices (affirming a broad range of experiences is the most helpful for

healing; a collective trauma impacts individuals differently, particularly those who have different economic resources or are in marginalized subcommunities);

3 Re-establishing the rhythms and routines of life and engaging in collective healing rituals; and
4 Arriving at a positive vision of the future with renewed hope.

Seen through a prism of Christian practice, these four themes touch on ways of being and doing that are part of normal church life: fellowship, pastoral care and listening, engaging with the Word and sacrament, worship and living into the future with eyes on the commonwealth of God. Saul's emphasis on engaging collaboratively with the whole community encourages the type of church leadership that draws on the ministry of the baptized, enabling the whole people of God to find the way forward through the valley of the shadow.

As the Covid-19 pandemic tore through the world, religious leaders and churches were hampered in utilizing the resources at the heart of their life together as church buildings were closed and face-to-face public worship was made unavailable for months at a time. In response, congregations drew on their resources and continued their life together in forms old and new depending on their culture and their context: through mailings and email, online worship and Zoom coffee hours, offering their buildings for emergency services such as food banks. Leaders sought to keep people connected and resourced. Perseverance and innovation paired to keep the boat afloat in the storm and may have the effect of changing church life for some for ever.

Other attributes of collective trauma

There are other features of collective trauma that impact the journey of recovery. Drawing on what we learned in Part 1, we know that individuals in a community or congregation will be impacted in a range of ways and that recovery will be uneven.

The diversity of responses will require sensitive handling in order to move forward together. What works for some will not work for all. An array of pastoral responses will be needed along with the flexibility to change course if something is not working.

Trauma breaks down inhibitions. After a traumatizing event expect an increased number of divorces and births, increased domestic violence and increased addictive behaviours (alcohol, drugs, sex, shopping). Individuals with pre-existing mental health conditions may find those exacerbated. So too people who have been previously traumatized in similar ways may be strongly impacted: the resurgence of Black Lives Matter on a global scale in 2020 after the killing of George Floyd resulted in strong triggered reactions as embodied memories of racial attacks and discrimination coursed through the bodies of those who had experienced racism. Gay men and others vulnerable to the AIDS/HIV epidemic in the 1980s and 1990s may have found that the 2020 Covid-19 pandemic triggered traumatic responses. A church or community will have more vulnerable people and additional safeguarding concerns.

Collective traumas are also revelatory. Less looked at aspects of the community are revealed as the veil is torn, some of it very difficult to look at. The Covid-19 pandemic revealed much: the scope of global interdependence as a sneeze in Wuhan, China became a worldwide pandemic causing over two million deaths and counting; a hierarchy of valuation where workers identified as 'essential' (in care, food distribution and transport) nonetheless earn very low wages; the link between structural inequality and serious illness and death, particularly in black, Asian and minority ethnic communities; the robustness (or lack thereof) of health care delivery systems; and the capacity of governments to manage national catastrophe. Untold numbers of research projects will poke and prod the experience of 2020 and beyond for lessons to be learned.

Not only are collective traumas revelatory in this way, but it is not unusual for a community trauma to bring about a great uncovering of seemingly unrelated problems. A traumatizing event shakes the foundations and other cracks are exposed. The revelation of the misconduct of a church leader destabilizes the congregation and allegations of embezzlement or other misdoings by other leaders emerge. A pandemic roars through the nations and the festering wound of systemic racism is exposed.[6] Trauma is the unasked-for gift that just keeps giving.

We turn next to pastoral and leadership strategies.

Key takeaway points

- A community or congregation is traumatized when either significant or a significant number of individuals are traumatized by a particular event, or when the structure and assumptive framework of the group is damaged in life-threatening ways to some.
- Fundamental assumptions about the world and life are shattered in trauma.
- There are phases a community or congregation move through as it recovers from a traumatizing event: from heroism through disillusionment to rebuilding and restoration, and hopefully to a wiser living phase. The journey can take from two to five years or more after a one-off traumatizing event.
- Collective trauma calls for a collective recovery response, engaging as many people in the group as possible and accounting for diverse experiences.
- Each community's journey of recovery will be unique but best includes rebuilding and building on relationships, telling the story of the community's experience and response, collective healing rituals and the restoration of the rhythms of life, and eventually being able to hold a hopeful vision for the future.
- Trauma is disinhibiting, leading to more vulnerability and possibly further traumatizing revelations about the community.

Notes

1 In religious terms these translate to 1) God is sovereign, 2) God can be trusted to be benevolent, and 3) God loves me (Ganzevoort 2009, pp. 188–9).

2 For the story of the creation of this ICTG chart (reproduced with permission), see 'Healing Trajectory Charts – a brief history', www.ictg.org/phases-of-disaster-response.html, accessed 1.06.2020. As noted on the ICTG website, the graph is an adaptation of others available elsewhere.

3 Institute for Collective Trauma and Growth, ICTG Chart 'Phase details – which phase are you in right now?', www.ictg.org/phases-of-disaster-response.html, accessed 1.06.2020.

4 Dr Sarah Horsman, conversation with the Tragedy and Congregations team.

5 Southgate (2019b, pp. 122–33) draws on James F. Hopewell's 1987 *Congregation: Stories and Structures*, Philadelphia, PA: Fortress Press, to explore how congregations respond to traumatizing events out of their internal narratives.

6 See Menakem (2017) for an exploration of the trauma that is the original wound that begets and engenders racism. Menakem offers practices aimed at healing both black and white people.

9

Picking Up the Pieces:
Pastoral Responses to
Collective Trauma

In this chapter and the next three we will consider pastoral and liturgical resources and strategies to help a congregation move through the journey of post-trauma recovery. It is good to keep in mind that trauma is held in the body. Therefore some strategies are bodily. Trauma impacts individuals and communities. Wise leaders employ both individual and collective strategies. Trauma leaves one feeling powerless and helpless. Our strategies seek to connect people to their natural resources and provide other possible resources, respecting and supporting the agency and autonomy of those who have been traumatized. Finally, trauma is about the impact of having lost meaningful things – loss of loved ones, a home, a job, one's understanding of how the world works or basic assumptions about self and God and life. Thus our strategies are also about facilitating sense- and meaning-making, piecing together shattered understandings and creating a more resilient narrative that can hold the fact that terrible things happen.

The role of church leadership is to marshal and utilize resources for the care of self, others and the community; to reconnect people to their resources; to work to heal and nurture the system so that it may become more functional; and finally to hold the larger story of the community and enable the integration of the traumatizing event into it.

Pastoral and liturgical strategies should go hand in hand: strategies for the care of the individual and of the community can support or undermine each other. Pastoral needs may dictate what happens in worship. Appropriate liturgy provides a container for healing for both the individual and the community. As you read through these chapters you may make many connections.

This chapter focuses on pastoral strategies. Recall the habits of the heart that were identified in Part 1. These habits will help congregations and individuals to survive, adapt and grow in the aftermath of a traumatizing event. The Three C's – calming, communication and caring – shape the responses the leadership team creates in every phase. And the compassionate discipline of self-care enables leaders to give their best under trying circumstances over the long haul.

Pastoral care in the heroic phase

Acute pastoral care is covered in Part 1, Chapters 4 and 5. The principles of care set out in those chapters are also helpful in every phase of the journey of recovery:

- OMG strategies for people who are showing a triggered traumatic response
- Normalization after careful listening (*what you are feeling is normal for a person who has gone through what you have gone through; what we are experiencing is normal for a community that has been through what we have been through*)
- Connecting people to their resources
- Watchful waiting
- 'The survivor is the expert'
- Resonant care (warmth plus precision)
- Assuring that carers are cared for, and
- Referring the few who have severe and persistent symptoms of post-traumatic stress.

Pastoral care in the disillusionment phase

The disillusionment phase comes with its own set of pastoral challenges. Recall the information in Chapter 7 (Superheroes): self-care is a priority. Days off are not optional if you want to be able to help your community throughout the long haul. Do whatever you need to keep healthy and resourced – even if you do not feel like it. Especially if you do not feel like it. Keep a healthy boundary between work and life. Take regular breaks each day. Schedule a holiday for three to six months' time and pay for it. If a holiday is in the diary and prepaid, you will be more likely to take it. This may be difficult to do especially if others have lost loved ones, homes or jobs, but it is crucial. The work is costly. You must make and take opportunities for rest and renewal or you may do harm as well as good. It is not unusual for church leaders involved in traumatic events to experience illness, burnout or vocational trauma in the aftermath.

Leadership during the disillusionment phase calls for self-regulation which is always easier when one is resourced and rested. Being non-reactive in the face of disparaging remarks, percolating conflicts and unpredictable outbursts will enable you to be a container for some of the negative energy that leeches out through this time. Your capacity to tolerate and hold strong and negative feelings and their expression will help the community accept and grapple with what has happened. People need to be able to say and be how they really are. When negative emotions are expressed, they are subjected to light and air and people may then be able to move on from them. It is the old adage: the only way through the pain is *through* the pain, not around or avoiding it. The non-reactive leader can engage with diverse emotions and issues and express what they feel and believe while maintaining emotional connection with those who may disagree. Bridge Builders offers three C's for the leading of an anxious (traumatized or hurting) congregation: Calm, Curiosity and Connection. The calm, curious, connected leader leans in towards disagreeable or disagreeably expressed feelings or opinions with curiosity.[1]

Individual pastoral care strategies are set out in Chapter 5 (Care That Heals). What does communal pastoral care look like? First it looks like the ministry of the baptized – encouraging your congregation to offer its natural gifts to one another and beyond. Phone calls, cards, hugs, cakes; offers of shopping, a lift or child minding ... the ordinary ways of care are very powerful when a community has been traumatized. It has been delivered a body blow that shatters the sense of the goodness of the world and may sow seeds of distrust. Simple acts of paying attention and caring begin to restore trust. They also build the community's resilience and sense of agency and self-esteem.

An important theme in communal pastoral care during the disillusionment phase is *normalization* after careful listening: communicating that what people are feeling day to day (exhausted, confused, angry) is a normal response to a traumatizing event and that the congregation is on a journey of recovery that will include this difficult, low-energy, potentially conflictual time. The more people understand that what they are going through is normal, the easier it is for them to go through it.

Communal pastoral care invites the leadership to step back and think about the journey the community is making and how to facilitate it. Just as individuals are making their personal journeys through what is essentially a period of bereavement with all the chaos and strong feeling that may entail, so too is the community. The disillusionment phase is a wandering in the wilderness period. Be watchful, prayerful and discerning as to what might help the community hold together and eventually make meaning out of what has happened. Celebrate simple survival and adaptation. Some days just making it through the day will be an accomplishment.

Strategies to encourage and keep people connected include *social events and gatherings* that provide opportunities for just being together and maybe even light-hearted fun. Weeks after the Grenfell Tower fire, St Clement and St James pondered whether to continue with the church fête. It seemed disrespectful in the face of so much death and grief and there were logistical problems with the garden. But it was decided that the fête would go ahead and it ended up being a welcome respite in the midst of a tragic time.[2] These events provide a reprieve from the onslaught of pain and remind the community that joy has not abandoned them.

Small group meetings are also means of communal pastoral care. Facilitated debriefing meetings enable people to come together to express their thoughts and feelings. Prayer groups and Bible study groups enable people to form or sustain relationships, draw on their faith and other resources, support one another, and begin to make sense of what has happened and the journey they are making. Educational meetings that address the dynamics of trauma (using information from this book or other resources) or that relate specifically to the traumatizing event can be particularly helpful. For instance, it can be helpful in a case of clergy sexual abuse to provide information about the power dynamics between minister and church member and the impact of such abuse on the victims (which include the congregation), or, if a young person has killed themselves, education about mental health or suicide. Anything that will shed light on how or why something has happened enables greater calm and understanding.

Expect that anything you offer in terms of small or large group meetings may have to be repeated with information shared via different kinds of media. The disillusionment phase is low-energy and depressing and everyone is in a different place. Expecting a low turnout will help manage the discouragement.

If physical gathering is not possible (as it was not during the lockdown phases of the Covid-19 pandemic), there may be other ways to keep people connected and informed: group and individual online meetings, telephone check-ins, mass mailings or emailing, invitations to contribute lines that can be used to make a crowd-sourced poem or other participatory activities.

Returning to the traumatizing event

Sometimes the community may benefit from further attention to the trauma. These are the signs: it cannot be spoken of or it is all that is talked about (it has become the community's identity); high reactivity; people leaving; bizarre behaviour; displaced emotion; scapegoating. In the aftermath of a traumatizing event if the primary emotions of anger, fear or grief are not discharged by expression or action, secondary emotions emerge: whining, moaning, unresolved guilt, frustration, anger that doesn't lead to anything.

It may be difficult to persuade people to cycle back and spend some time discussing the originating trauma. When you meet resistance to this idea (or resistance to anything), meet with the resisters. Gently and respectfully say, 'Tell me more about how this is for you'. Try to understand where they are coming from. Be clear about your objectives. Stay emotionally connected, consider their concerns (which may cause you to adapt your approach or ideas) and then stand your ground.

If enough of the gathered community is willing to revisit the originating trauma, it is important to have a clear structure for the meeting and facilitation, which can be from within the community or may involve an external person brought in specially for the task. It also may help to have a group covenant addressing how the participants will be together. Here is a sample:

- Respectful listening without interrupting
- Speaking for oneself, not on behalf of others
- Confidentiality: share the learning, not the stories
- Take responsibility for what you share: if you feel uncomfortable to share something personal, do not do it.[3]

Facilitated meetings are opportunities to meet in the presence of God, whose sheltering embrace is lived out in the structure and care with which the meeting is conducted. Beginning with prayer, a hymn and a Bible reading, the plenary leader can offer input before the gathering breaks out into small facilitated groups, followed by a plenary sharing of the discussions. The final five minutes can include a What's Next reflection and prayer. See Appendix D for a sample meeting outline.

In the appendices you will also find Appendix E, a facilitator's checklist that reminds the breakout group facilitators of their primary tasks and tools. Facilitators are people who are able to remain calm, curious and connected when the heat rises. The aims of facilitation are to listen to understand what people are feeling and thinking and to make sure that everyone who wants to contribute to the conversation may do so. These are accomplished by paying attention to group dynamics – who needs to be encouraged to speak and who needs to listen more – and by promoting acceptance of difference. People may be reluctant to express opinions or feelings they fear no one else holds. But the reality is that there are usually diverse perspectives in a room. Hearing those perspectives strengthens a community and enables movement together. As Ruth Layzell (2019, p. 204) writes,

> where the events can be spoken of frankly and accurately in public (within the bounds of confidentiality) and a wide range of responses (e.g. numbness, anger, outrage, guilt, despair, helplessness) acknowledged as normal, understanding may be increased and permission given for that range of felt responses, opening the way for conversations to continue which express rather than deny the impact so that the necessary process of what has happened can take place. This works against the tendency for trauma to silence voices or for certain reactions to go underground and ... enhances the possibility for mutual support and compassion.

The facilitator's tools include:

- Self-regulation
- Calmness
- Clarity about purpose and role
- 'Please say more' (curiosity to explore what is behind people's statements)

- Summarization: if someone makes a provocative or emotionally evocative statement, after saying 'please say more' to seek to understand it, summarization of what was heard (e.g. 'So you are concerned that ...' or 'So your past experience leads you to ...')

This last technique helps to defuse the emotions in the statement and to place the responsibility of that statement where it belongs – with the person who made it and who may be speaking and acting out of an unspoken hurt or fear.

No matter how sensitively you have prepared and implemented an event there may still be some thoughts and feelings that will not be expressed publicly. Layzell (2019, p. 204) offers this wisdom:

> Some things are too personal, private and particular, too much out of step with everyone else or felt to be too shameful – or simply not ready yet to emerge from the inchoate sensory knowing of the limbic system to the more cognitive awareness of the cerebral cortex. So space and silence within corporate worship, to gather those who might otherwise be alienated and to contain what cannot yet come to voice, are vital for a very long time [after a traumatizing event] (arguably always, since leaders of worship can never know all of what those joining the congregation may be experiencing).

Blame and forgiveness

Certain kinds of traumatizing events elicit such great discomfort that energy arises to deny the traumatic impact, to blame the victims, or to press for forgiveness and moving on.

Denial, scapegoating and victim-blaming protect the fundamental assumptions Janoff-Bulmann identified, discussed in the previous chapter. These kinds of responses are particularly common in cases of clergy sexual misconduct and may even be a necessary first stage in the recovery process (Grosch-Miller 2019b, pp. 245–7). Congregations are emotional systems and, like all emotional systems, will tend towards preserving the status quo. It is unbearable for some to believe that a religious leader – who perhaps married them, buried their parent or baptized their child – would commit such an egregious betrayal of trust. So they will rise up quickly to defend their minister. In the short run it is important that people have the opportunity to vent their anger and pain in a safe enough environment. But where scapegoating and victim-blaming continue, the environment is made unsafe for others and the need for careful facilitation is all the greater. In the long run victim-blaming prevents people from grappling with what has happened. It also results in poorer outcomes for victims/survivors, the congregation and even the alleged offender.

While confrontation will not be effective soon after allegations have been revealed and people are traumatized by the information, at some point blaming the victim must be addressed. It may be helpful for people to know that victim-blaming is normal when things like this happen. And the congregation needs gently to be reminded that the source of their hurt is a result of the minister's conduct and not because victims have come forward or because a spouse was not paying attention.[4] This is a message that will have to be given sensitively and possibly repeatedly without demonizing the offender or their supporters. The aim is to accord all involved – the alleged perpetrator, the victims, impacted family members – with dignity and pastoral care and support. That will aid the congregation in its recovery. Recall too the earlier chapter on moral injury (Chapter 6); there may be those who will be severely impacted and need particular care.

Pressure to forgive and to move on is common in the disillusionment phase. This may be a form of denial, seeking to avoid the pain of what has happened. Or it could be that some people have metabolized the trauma, made sufficient sense of what has happened and are ready to move on before others have done so. In the former case the congregation needs the reminder that the only way to recover and grow from a painful event is to face into the pain and give it expression. In the latter case the leader's task is to help people understand that everyone will not be making the journey of recovery at the same pace or in the same way. To move together requires patience on the part of those who have processed the trauma. In both cases it is important to address the question of forgiveness.

Forgiveness is an essential element of the Christian faith. We pray for it in the Lord's Prayer: 'forgive us our sins, as we forgive those who sin against us'. Many Christians believe that forgiveness is what was accomplished on the cross. If people are pressing for forgiveness it is an opportunity for preaching and small group work that more fully explores this key part of faithful living. It will be helpful for people to understand that forgiveness is a journey that cannot be forced; pressuring an individual or group to forgive impedes the journey and delays the possibility of forgiveness. True reconciliation includes accountability as well as compassion.

Pastoral strategies for rebuilding and restoration

Eventually comes the rebuilding phase, when the congregation will have turned a corner and most people have accepted that the terrible thing happened and that the world is not all bad. Hearts begin to dare to hope and people turn their vision towards what now can be done to rebuild the community. While there may still be grief and difficult times there is also new energy and initiative. The general mood is one of possibility as creativity is sparked and sustained. The difficult moments are not as debilitating or long-lasting.

Individuals will continue to be moving at their own pace so people will be in different places in the journey of recovery. They will also have different understandings and interpretations of what happened. Communal pastoral care in this phase seeks to help the community to *hold diversity*. In any group there will be different thoughts and feelings about any event, even among people who live together or are related. The Bible itself holds conflicting narratives: prosperity theology sits alongside *sell all your goods and give to the poor*; Israel is admonished to treat the stranger as a citizen and later foreign wives are divorced and banished. The mind of Christ that we seek to share is not so much agreement in all things but learning to disagree respectfully within the heart of Christ while seeking to discern the way ahead. As you invite your congregation to acknowledge and embrace that not everyone is the same, you are building strength and resilience. You are helping people to mature in their understanding of how human beings are and how the church can be unified while diverse. You are also facilitating discernment and decision-making: a church makes better decisions if there is a range of perspectives in the room interacting respectfully.

While people will have been attempting to make sense of what happened and to integrate it into the story of their lives and their life together, this work can now be more intentional. Human beings are storytelling creatures. Storytelling is how our brains function to make sense of self and to make meaning of the experiences of life. When we are traumatized our capacity to do that is temporarily suspended. In the disillusionment phase energy is low and the mood is despairing. Now, though, that life is looking a bit more balanced, the task of *reframing the story* moves to the fore. Our framework for understanding life has been assaulted and needs to be reconstructed to account for the possibility of events like this. More will be said about the reframing task in the chapters on worship (Chapter 12) and the creation of a new story (Chapter 13) as worship will be a container for much of that work. Outside of worship, communal pastoral care can facilitate this reframing. Prayer groups, Bible study and fellowship are natural arenas for people to converse about where they see God at work. The reframing happens organically, inchoately, intuitively as the church does what it always has done – worships, serves, prays and praises; learns, listens and looks for the movement of the Spirit.

Janoff-Bulman (1992, pp. 95ff) observes that the natural process of rebuilding shattered assumptions is difficult and painful. It is facilitated by three different coping processes in the individual: 1) automatic routines for processing the new powerful data of the traumatizing event, specifically denial, numbing and intrusive re-experiencing; 2) efforts to re-interpret or massage the new data so that it fits better into the old assumptions; and 3) interactions with others. Through these processes an attempt is made to understand the event in a way that maximizes being able to perceive the world as benevolent and meaningful and the self as worthy of esteem. This helps to re-establish cognitive stability and emotional well-being (Janoff-Bulman 1992, pp. 117–18).

Early on after a traumatizing event the first coping process is prevalent. A person may experience an oscillation between numbing and uncontrollable re-experiencing. The numb periods give the brain a rest; when it is ready, re-experiencing emerges. These states alternate as the brain automatically attempts to come to terms with and make sense of what has happened. The second coping process – massaging the new information – is seen in phenomena like scapegoating and blaming the victim. In time it may become necessary for a church leader to challenge these to enable a more functional re-interpretation for community well-being. The third coping process of interacting with others can be seen operating when individuals a) compare themselves with others who were more tragically impacted by the event, b) blame themselves for the event thereby minimizing its malevolence and randomness, or c) find benefits and purpose in the event, a kind of 'lessons learned' strategy (Janoff-Bulman 1992, p. 118). These types of coping happen in conversation with self and with others as people tell the story again and again. Narration is how the mind confronts, reconsiders and integrates a traumatizing experience. By telling the story the person takes control of it and works with it.

Any and all of these coping processes will be at work in a community in the aftermath of a traumatizing event. Communal pastoral care to support the healthy use of these processes includes normalizing that people will be in different places and that good and bad days (alternating states of rest and alarm) will occur; being aware and alert to self-blame that is functional when it addresses unhelpful behaviours and self-blame that is characterological (assuming the self is bad) and unhelpful; and supporting or encouraging constructive reflection.

Reframing – making meaning from – a collective loss is a

collective task. Public opportunities for collective reflection during which all voices are welcomed and encouraged are important. To be unheard or excluded is invalidating for individuals and subgroups and undermines communal health and well-being. People need to feel they can share their experiences. Saul (2014, p. 134) notes that the necessity for collective reflection is particularly important when the traumatizing event is history-making.

A final communal pastoral strategy to build the strength and resilience of your community is to *gather wisdom*. Be alert to opportunities to glean the learnings of this period. You and your congregation will gain things through this experience. Every one of the clergypersons interviewed for the Tragedies and Congregations project found gifts in the situation as they and their congregations rose to meet the challenge, while regretting the high cost of those gifts. Notice and celebrate the positive things that come about, never denying the tragedy of the great loss. As you do this you are reinforcing that the church is a learning community – an attribute that will serve the church all of its days.

When the trauma is complex, unfolding and ongoing

Complex collective trauma wears people and communities down. When another shock to the system appears, there will be less heroism to go around. Disillusionment may drag on and on as energy is sapped in the face of a lack of safety and security. It is important to recognize that no one and nothing will be functioning optimally. We must cut ourselves and others plenty of slack, lower the goalposts of achievement, and celebrate making it through the day, the week, the month.

Again and always, self-care is not optional. We need to practise it and to model it. Chronic stress will take its toll on us and on those around us. I wrote briefly about strategies to manage chronic stress in Chapter 7 (Superheroes): physical exercise, life-giving spiritual practices, connecting with loved ones and learning something new. Mental rest is necessary for a brain overwhelmed with trying to cope. As well as increasing the positive things that restore us, reducing those tasks or expectations which are draining will give us breathing space.

Encouraging attention to basic human needs, including physical and mental health needs, will dominate leadership tasks when a collective trauma persists, shaping ministry and mission. Recall Maslow's hierarchy of needs (Chapter 4).

Managing in a complex, unfolding collective trauma is like running a marathon. Pace yourself. Fuel your body, mind and soul often. Be present to the moment and take frequent breaks. Steward your resources. Remind yourself: human beings are made to be adaptable. We can do this.

Key takeaway points

- Collective loss calls for collective responses while also attending to individual pastoral care needs.
- Pastoral care strategies in the disillusionment phase include self-care and self-regulation; normalization; affirming survival and adaptation; social events and gatherings; small group work (educational and spiritual).
- There may be a need to revisit the traumatizing event.
- Denial, scapegoating, victim-blaming or pressure to forgive may need to be addressed.
- Pastoral care strategies in the rebuilding and restoration phase include acknowledging and accepting diversity as part of unity; reframing the story of what happened and rebuilding shattered assumptions; gathering wisdom.

Notes

1 Bridge Builders (www.bbministries.org.uk) offers training to strengthen the ministry of Christian leaders by helping them to be more self-aware and to develop greater skills, confidence and resilience for working with tensions and conflict in Christian communities. They offer a course called 'Leading in Anxious Times – A Systems Approach to Leadership', which includes these three C's.

2 The Revd Alan Everett, conversation with Tragedies and Congregations team.

3 Thank you to Sandra Cobbin from Bridge Builders who offered these in a workshop for interim ministers titled 'Family Systems: Managing a Big, Anxious Family', 1 October 2019.

4 Female victims and female spouses of offending male clergy are often blamed for a minister's sexual misconduct (Grosch-Miller 2019b, pp. 245–7).

10

Crying Out Loud:
The Lost Art of Lamentation

This chapter bridges the previous chapter on communal pastoral care and the next chapters on the Bible and liturgy and worship. Lamentation will be seen to be a profoundly pastoral and liturgical strategy and art.

In cultures throughout recorded time there appear to be three traditional types of songs: lullabies, wedding songs and laments (Lee 2010, p. 7). One of the earliest literary texts available to us is the 'Lament to the Spirit of War' written by the Sumerian poet priestess Enheduanna over 4,300 years ago (Lee 2010, pp. 27–30). The power of lamentation to articulate and transform the deep pain and longing of a people cannot be underestimated. In traumatizing times lamentation can be a tool that enables people to unite around pain and move through it.

The biblical witness underscores the power of lamentation. From Rachel's cry (Jeremiah 31.15) to Job's accusations, from the book of Lamentations to the Psalms, from the disciples crying out in the storm to Jesus crying out from the cross, the Bible testifies to the faithful exercise of full-throated pleas of pain, anger and fear addressed to God. When we are at the end of our tether, helpless and afraid, we turn to the source of our life and our life together. As John Swinton (2009, p. 104) observes: 'Lament takes the brokenness of human experience into the heart of God and demands that God answer'. I would add: in lamentation we enter the broken heart of God.

In the next chapter we will look at how ritual and worship facilitate the journey of post-traumatic recovery and growth.

A key element is that they provide a container that holds, structures and forms human experience. So it is for lamentation. A lament can hold the strong and disturbing emotions of a traumatized person or community in a safe enough space for people to be present to their embodied experience and to begin to move through it. In other words, lamentation frames the liminal space that facilitates crossing the threshold from one state of being (alarmed, enraged, hurting) to another (asking, hoping, praying). Our praying refigures the trauma; our imaginations begin to transform by placing our lives in God's hands (Jones 2009, p. 53).

Psalms of lament

Prayers of lament make a strong showing and have a particular function in the book of Psalms. Walter Brueggemann (1984, pp. 19–21) observes that the Psalter reflects the reality of human experience: that human life has periods of relative stability and well-being (orientation), disrupted by events or seasons of alienation, suffering, pain or death (disorientation), occasioning the necessity for re-stabilizing that can include surprising gifts from God (new orientation).[1] He organizes his discussion of the psalms roughly into these three categories: psalms of orientation, psalms of disorientation and psalms of new orientation. Psalms of lament fall into the middle category and perform the middle function of enabling movement towards a new orientation.

While diverse commentators categorize the psalms in slightly different ways and some psalms are mixed genre, what is most remarkable about the Psalter, the ancient prayerbook of the Hebrew people, is that the largest category are psalms of lament, individual and communal. They make up roughly one-third of the book of Psalms, a larger proportion than hymns of praise or psalms of thanksgiving. And yet they are the least represented genre in the Revised Common Lectionary. Christian worship in the West has moved these psalms to the margins, uncomfortable with the strong, negative emotions expressed, with curses and cries for vengeance. Sunday worship has been sanitized, the psalms of lament edited or excised entirely as if that part of being human is not fit to present to God. And yet the biblical witness is strong. Our ancestors in faith engaged in a real and raw relationship with God: honest, fierce and struggling.

Brueggemann, Swinton and others grieve the loss of lamentation in Christian worship. The consequence, say Billman and Migliore (2006, p. 42), is that our prayer is

> alienated from the biblical tradition, cut off from the cries of suffering people in our congregations, society, and around the world, and deaf to the groaning of the whole creation so gravely endangered today by human abuse and exploitation.

We forget how to hold strong negative emotion and that God is large and merciful and able to hold it with and for us. We forgo the language of suffering when we are most in need of it.

You may remember that a traumatized person may lose the power of speech. There are no words. There is no way to begin to process what has happened. As the shock wears off, the disjoined way that memory is stored (or not stored) in trauma continues to contribute to the difficulty of finding words for the experience. Here a psalm of lament offers a language and a structure that begins to order the chaos. Here the prayerbook of the ancient Hebrews may become the voice of suffering humanity once again. From the psalms we learn the depth of prayer and the art of lamentation.

What lamentation offers to the traumatized person or community – whether it is from the Psalter or one written for the occasion – is the opportunity to begin to bridge their inner experience with their outer experience, giving voice to the pain and suffering that is witnessed by God and others. Recall the power of witness in the discussion of resonant care in Chapter 5. In lamentation the chaos of the situation is held in a safe and structured space, the isolating experience is shared and in some sense normalized, bonds of community are strengthened, and the heart takes the first tentative steps towards hope.

The structure of psalms of lament

The containing structure of the psalms of lament in its barest bones is this (Warner 2019a, p. 173):

- address to God ('O Lord, God of my salvation', Psalm 88.1a);
- complaint ('You have rejected us and abased us, and have not gone out with our armies. You made us turn back from the foe, and our enemies have taken spoil for themselves. You have made us like sheep for slaughter ... You have sold your people for a trifle ...', Psalm 44.9–12); and
- petition ('Restore our fortunes, O Lord, like the watercourses in the Negeb', Psalm 126.4).

The complaint – a detailed listing of what exactly is wrong, what God has done or failed to do – is the middle passage, the heartcry, the hurt. The petition – the turning towards God to ask or demand what needs to be done – is where hope is born. Sometimes accompanied by the recitation of past deliverance ('I will call to mind the deeds of the Lord; I will remember your wonders of old', Psalm 77.11), remembering how God has acted in the past and asking for help now plants the seeds for future hope and praise.

Other elements that appear in psalms of lament include:

- statements of trust in or relationship to God ('But I trust in you, O Lord; I say, "You are my God"', Psalm 31.14);
- curses ('May his children wander about and beg; may they be driven out of the ruins they inhabit. May the creditor seize all that he has; may strangers plunder the fruits of his toil ...', Psalm 109.10–11); and
- a vow of praise ('Hope in God; for I shall again praise him, my help and my God', Psalm 42.11b).

The existence of vows of praise in almost all of the psalms of lament (not Psalm 88) has given scholars pause to reflect. Despite blaming God for malfeasance or neglect, spilling bile and bitterness, the psalmist says, we will give thanks to your name for ever (Psalm 44.8). Warner (2019a, pp. 174–5) notes that the explanations for the strange and sometimes abrupt shifts of mood (see Psalm 13) range from liturgical and editorial to psychological. The vows could have been added at a later point in time or inserted for liturgical purposes. She observes that the most persuasive contemporary explanations for the swift turn to praise have been the psychological: that expressing the pain and distress enables the psalmist to will to praise again.[2] Recall the naming exercise offered in Chapter 2: when we articulate feelings, an internal shift happens that creates new neural pathways and further integrates the emotional and thinking parts of the brain.

As a twenty-first-century Christian I warm to the psychological explanation. When I was an ordinand working part-time in a church, my then six-year-old daughter would play after school in the well-appointed library in the basement of the church while I would work two floors above. One day in the car on the way home she said, 'Mr X had me sit on his lap and told me not to tell you.' You can imagine the explosion this sparked in my inner being. I breathed deeply and said, 'Thank you for telling me; that was the right thing. Tell me more.' I was determined not to lead the witness. From what she said it seemed he had begun the process of grooming her for more intimate contact. That night after I put her to bed, I stood in my lounge with my Bible open to the book of Job and gave God a piece of my mind (including some choice language): *How dare you let this happen? And I gave up my life to follow you?* You get the picture. After 20 minutes I laid down to sleep and I heard, *Did you expect to be immune from the world?* Now, had I been asked that question before this event, I would have said, *Of course not.* But deep within I was harbouring some unhelpful expectations about my life in God. My lamentation moved me from pain to humility.

As appealing as the psychological explanation is, however, I want to suggest that there may be a good liturgical and pastoral reason for including a vow of praise in some circumstances. If you are leading a communal lament, although some in the congregation may not be ready to vow praise, the strength of such a vow in the tradition argues that it should be included. The worship leader holds and embodies the whole of the Christian tradition. More than that, praise cements the move towards hope that the petition began. Its inclusion strengthens that move and signals the direction of travel. A caution: if you are working with an individual or small group it is essential that you listen for and respect where people are. The invitation to vow praise in a lament should never be forced. People will vow praise when they are ready to (recall the mantra: the survivor is the expert). The movement from despair to hope, from lament to praise, is a long journey and a struggle. It is never automatic, guaranteed or even complete (Billman and Migliore 2006, p. 150). Not for nothing were the people of God named Israel, those who struggle or strive with God (Genesis 32.28).

Containment, formation, agency and honesty

Lamentation not only holds the chaotic and disturbing roil of emotion for traumatized people, it also forms the faith journey for recovery. Serene Jones (2009, pp. 56–7) identifies three 'habits of imagination' recalled in the process of lamentation. These are related to assumptions that may or will have been shattered in the traumatizing event, as discussed in Chapter 8: that God is sovereign and loves us; that God receives our speech and can act; and that the person is an agent whose actions in the world matter. Lamentation begins to make possible the eventual rebuilding of shattered assumptions that is necessary for making sense of and integrating the event into the story of one's life or community.

The third habit, recalling that human beings have agency, is particularly important. Although lamentation looks like blaming someone else (God even) for what has happened, the articulation of pain and asking for relief is an act of agency. A person asserts a sense of self and self-esteem when they so speak. While traumatizing events cut us off from a sense of self and leave us feeling powerless, speaking rebuilds the connection and begins to restore the capacity to act. The individual's humanity is affirmed in the midst of a dehumanizing experience.

The most salient characteristic of the lament is that it is searingly honest. Lament is the ravaged heart's cry to the source of being, the inconsolable ranting that reaches out to demand an end to suffering, the fierce force of living in the face of death that turns towards God in resolute hope. The truthful nature of lament means that one cannot force or mandate lament. It is for the leader or pastoral carer to discern whether and how a person or community may be invited into lamentation. As with all responses seeking to facilitate post-traumatic recovery, context and the diversity of human response shape what is possible and what may work. For some people, a refusal to lament may be a necessary temporary defence (Billman and Migliore 2006, p. 18). Others may resist because they fear the downward movement of disillusionment and would prefer to avoid pain and skip to joy. A reminder that people will be in different places and that joint activity helps the whole group move through a difficult season will not be remiss.

The honesty of lamentation is fearful to some and attractive to others. The great German theologian Jürgen Moltmann (1974, pp. 4–5) traces the beginning of his faith to reading the book of Psalms in a Bible given to him while a prisoner of war in Scotland. Those psalms and Jesus' cry on the cross – *My God, my God, why have you forsaken me?* (Psalm 22) – recalled Moltmann to life. Jesus understood. The psalms were the words of Moltmann's own heart.

Invitation to lament

Lament tends to be most useful in the early phases of a collective trauma, before the impetus of energy has begun to focus on restoration and rebuilding.[3] If you determine that an invitation to lament is what is called for, Swinton (2009, pp. 127–8) provides a helpful structure, derived from the contemporary psalmist and poet Ann Weems and here expanded:

1 Address God, using any names or titles that speak to you or express qualities of God that you want to call upon.
2 Make your complaints – be detailed. What has happened? Who is hurting and why? Whose fault is it? Give God the full blast of your anger, hurt and fear.
3 Express trust in or relationship with God. This can be one sentence. See, for example, Lamentations 3.24: '"The LORD is my portion," says my soul, "therefore I will hope in him".'
4 Make an appeal or petitions ... a request for God's intervention and why it is needed.
5 Vow your praise. Terrible things have happened *and yet* I will praise you.

The Tragedy and Congregations team included a lament-writing session in teaching clergy and ordinands and found it a formative and impactful practice. While never asking people to share what they had written, the team did ask what the experience of writing was like. Often it was reported back that something shifted, some opening movement occurred unexpectedly and was received gratefully.

Lament as protest

Lamentation not only plays a part in enabling post-traumatic recovery. It also makes way for the coming of the new day.

Brueggemann (2014) identifies three prophetic tasks in a cataclysm: face reality; embrace grief; find hope. Lament as protest is the middle transit, the liminal practice that enables what is revealed and what is lost to be railed against and grieved and opens the way to the creation of a better world. It is a practice that subverts and resists evil and suffering, unsettles the balance of power and creates new possibilities.

Slaves in Egypt raise their voices to the sky. God hears. Moses takes off his sandals. God says: 'I have observed the misery of my people ... I have heard their cry ... I have come down to deliver them' (Exodus 3.7–8). A voice is heard in Ramah. Rachel is inconsolable. Her children have been killed or carried off into exile. God says: there is a reward for your work ... there is hope for your future (Jeremiah 31.15–17).

Lamentation – crying out in pain – is a 'visceral announcement that things are not right' (Brueggemann 2001, p. 11). Grief shatters denial. The capacity to grieve makes possible the dismantling of evil structures and the beginning of the new day. As I write this in the middle of the Covid-19 pandemic and the Black Lives Matter protests, no word has ever seemed more true.[4]

Parker Palmer (2000, pp. 30–6) makes the point that the movements that transform ourselves and our world come about when people who have been oppressed and marginalized refuse to live the half-life offered them and stand up to protest injustice. In the soil of dashed hope and broken dreams, battered bodies and fed-up souls, seeds of hope are planted that promise the coming reign of God's justice and peace.

Key takeaway points

- Lamentation is a liminal activity that helps people and communities move from pain towards hope.
- Important characteristics of a lament are the voicing of pain, truth-telling, being witnessed (by God and others), a containing structure, the assertion of agency and the nascent articulation of hope.
- The essential elements of a lament are address to God, complaint and petition. Additional elements that may be found are a statement of trust in or relationship to God and a vow of praise.
- Lamentation is most helpful in the early phases of a collective trauma.
- Lamentation not only aids post-traumatic recovery but can serve as a protest, subverting and resisting evil and suffering.

Notes

1 The movement described by Brueggemann parallels the ICTG chart in Chapter 8.

2 See also Strawn (2016, pp. 143–60), who describes praying the psalms of lament as potentially therapeutic and possibly fostering post-traumatic growth.

3 Billman and Migliore (2006, p. 110) offer these psalms for particular circumstances:

- Abandonment by friends or even God, Psalm 22
- Mourning a suicide, Psalm 88
- Ravages of illness and old age, Psalm 38
- Sense of defeat or discouragement, Psalm 69
- Suffering of abuse and other injustices, Psalm 55.

4 Lamentation enjoyed a revival during the pandemic. See Wright (2020), Brueggemann (2020) and Ward (2020). The latter echoes the call to lamentation in response to the climate crisis. I include as Appendix F my own 'Lament for a Time of Global Trauma'.

11

The Bible:
A Trauma Treasure Trove

If the Bible were a person, it would be a person bearing scars, plated broken bones, muscle tears, and other wounds of prolonged suffering ... This person would certainly have known joys and everyday life, but she or he also would bear in body and heart, the wisdom of centuries of trauma. He or she would know the truth of trauma and survival of it ... that person would not be pretty to look at. We might be tempted to avert our eyes. But for most of us, there will be a time when we need that person's wisdom. (Carr 2014, p. 250)

In 597 BC, Babylonian King Nebuchadnezzar II and his armies laid siege to Jerusalem, imprisoned King Jehoiachin and carried off the temple treasures, the royal family and 8,000 artisans, smiths and strong men back to Babylon. Zedekiah was installed as king of the now vassal state. This first siege of Jerusalem is recounted in 2 Kings 24.10–18.

The forced 'peace' broke and Zedekiah rebelled, with the result that in 589 BC Nebuchadnezzar brought all his might to bear in the second siege of Jerusalem. 2 Kings 25 briefly describes the horrors of that siege which lasted roughly two years: severe famine, the slaughter of the king's sons before his eyes after which they blinded him, the burning of the Temple and destruction and looting of its fabric, the annihilation of the king's residence and all the houses of Jerusalem, the destruction of the city's defensive walls, and the carrying off of most of those who had survived. The poorest people of the land were left behind to dress the vines and till the soil.

The brief half-chapter in 2 Kings is the only account of the destruction of Jerusalem and the exile of many of her people in the Bible. Yet this event so shaped the consciousness of the Judean people that its influence is considered by some to be seen in almost every book of the Hebrew Bible, the Christian Old Testament (Carr 2014, p. 76). In the decades after the destruction of the city and after the return to Jerusalem of some of the captives from 538 BC onwards, people wrestled to understand what had happened and how it could be that God's dwelling place and God's city could be so devastated.

A handful of writings are notably a direct response to the catastrophe. The prophet Jeremiah stayed in the city in 586 BC until forced to flee to Egypt in 582 BC in a third deportation. His writings and those of his younger contemporary Ezekiel, who was carried away to Babylon in the first siege, were produced early in the exile. Lamentations, which mourns the destruction of Jerusalem, is thought to be the voice of those who remained. The story of Daniel, also taken to Babylon where he is said to have served the royal court, was written in the second century BC long after the devastation and is thought to offer historical fictions about that period. Isaiah 40—55 (Deutero-Isaiah) with its message of comfort and introduction of the suffering servant hails from the conclusion of the exile as King Cyrus of Persia authorized the people's return to Jerusalem. Ezra and Nehemiah returned later; those books tell the long story of the rebuilding of the Temple and walls and the repopulation of the city.

Not only were physical structures eventually rebuilt, but deep wrestling about the nature of God, God's relationship with the people and the nation's identity resulted in theological rebuilding and innovation over the decades after the cataclysm. Like trauma survivors in every age, the people struggled to make sense and meaning of what had happened, to rebuild shattered assumptions and to integrate the events of the sixth century BC into the story of who they were and who they may become. The process of such sense- and meaning-making will be further explored in Part 3. The current chapter is interested in the results of such efforts, delved into by biblical scholars in recent decades who have looked at the Bible through the lens of trauma theory (Carr 2014; Boase and Frechette 2016).

While Jeremiah and the others show a direct response to the horrors, the remaining books of the Old Testament bear less obvious marks to the untrained eye. Over the years after the destruction of Jerusalem, the Judean exiles and their descendants looked back at their stories of origin, shaping and reimagining the Abraham cycle to give meaning and hope to the exiles (Carr 2014, pp. 42ff).[1] The smaller southern kingdom of Judah and its capital Jerusalem took on the history and identity of the larger northern kingdom of Israel which was destroyed in the eighth century BC by the Assyrians, a fate Judah had escaped then (Carr 2014, p. 122). With new eyes and a changed vista in the aftermath of trauma, the rest of the Torah was reshaped to reflect the exilic and post-exilic themes of self-blame, survival, chosen-ness and the need for purity to prevent another catastrophe (Carr 2014, pp. 127ff).

Importantly, God became God of all the earth not just the land of Israel and Judah, an idea first mooted by Hosea in the eighth century BC in Israel (Carr 2014, pp. 24–39) and developed further in Deutero-Isaiah. The destruction of God's dwelling place and city did not mean that Yahweh was defeated or weak. Yahweh could use a foreign king (Cyrus) to serve the divine purpose. In Ezekiel, the glory of the Lord can appear to the people in their displacement. Risen from the ashes of devastation, monotheism became the hallmark of the faith of those who became the People of the Book (Jews, Christians and Muslims).

The story of the people that was told to be able to encompass the reality of the destruction of the Temple and city was one of punishment for failing to honour the covenant with YHWH. As Serene Jones observed, 'For many who suffer deeply, the only thing that frightens them more than the idea that God is punishing them is the idea that God is not in charge at all' (Carr 2014, p. 32). Self-blame offers the reassurance that if one does the right thing, one will not be violated. The returning Judean exiles saw themselves as the true Israel, having survived and been given a second chance to get it right (Carr 2014, p. 130).

God survived the destruction of Jerusalem as God; punishment was understood as God's covenantal responsibility (Balentine 2016, p. 170). And after the return the story was retold again to emphasize the everlasting nature of the covenant and the possibility of forgiveness for a people who had a hard time keeping the law (Warner 2019b, p. 90).

The New Testament too is marked by trauma. In the Gospels the story of Jesus is told by trauma survivors after the crucifixion and retold in the wake of the destruction of the second Temple (Carr 2014, pp. 225ff). Paul's traumatizing encounter on the road to Damascus set him off on a journey that created Christianity as we know it, a journey that occasioned more traumatic events and included struggling with his earlier persecution of the Followers of the Way of Jesus (Clark 2016, pp. 231–47). The collection of New Testament writings concludes with the Revelation to John, the product of persecution of Christians by either Nero or Domitian.

What does it matter that our sacred texts are battle-scarred, muscle torn and limping, a kind of disaster and survival literature? Megan Warner (2019b, pp. 83–90) gives four reasons for valuing the traumatic origins of the Bible: 1) the text is robust, coming out of real-life experience with the worst that life can throw at an individual or community; 2) the Bible tells us we are not alone – while the experience of trauma is isolating, the Bible introduces us to companions who have been there, done that, got the t-shirt; 3) the text offers a language and a literature of suffering, most eloquently when we have lost the power of speech and most powerfully in the psalms of lament; and 4) the Bible models resilience, including the witness of how reframing the story makes meaning and builds strength. The resilience of the texts themselves, and of the faiths of the People of the Book, testify to the power of facing into and wrestling the chaos and suffering of difficult times.

When a community experiences senseless violence, betrayal or natural disaster; when the rug is pulled out and unnamed assumptions are shattered; when only the night sky is big enough to hold the enveloping darkness, biblical texts prove a trustworthy resource to navigate the long journey of wilderness wandering. Like stars in that darkness, the cross of Christ, the argument of Job, the tears of Jeremiah, the curses of the psalmist and the wisdom of Paul illumine the path towards Home.

Key takeaway points

* The Bible was significantly crafted and shaped through traumatic events.
* It is a robust, wise, eloquent, trustworthy and resilient companion.

Notes

1 Warner (2019b, pp. 81–91) observes that a high proportion of Genesis was composed after the return from exile: 'what appears to be an old, safe, family story is, in fact, a subversive political tract, intelligible to certain groups but opaque to Persian occupiers ...' (p. 84).

12

Liturgy and Worship: The Work of the People

> In the endless hours and bewildering days following trauma, worship holds the broken heart of the people. Ritual gives shape to the chaos of grief, anger and disbelief, weaving a journey through the valley of the shadow. (Kraus, Holyan and Wismer 2017, p. 20)

Public worship is a container for the work of trauma recovery from the earliest stages. It is the natural setting for the faith community: the place where it gathers in the presence of God to break open the Word, to share bread and life, and to open itself to the workings of the Holy Spirit. When the community is gathered it is participating in an ancient human activity that has nourished human life for untold generations. Rituals structure and facilitate movement through the basic transitions in a human life: birth and death, continuity and change, mortality and transcendence (Bowie 2006, p. 168). The importance of ritual in human life is underscored by a suggested etymology of the word 'liturgy' from the Greek *leitourgia* (*leitos*, a form of *laos*: people + *ergo*: work). Liturgy can be conceived of as the work of the people.

Anthropologists have studied ritual behaviours for over a century. Arnold van Gennep's *The Rites of Passage* (1909) is the foundational text in which he identified ritual as a three-part journey of separation from daily life, transition and re-entry into daily life. The structure also parallels the observations of Brueggemann (1984) about the psalms (orientation, disorientation and new orientation) and Judith Herman's three stages

of recovery after trauma: safety, remembering and mourning, and reconnection with ordinary life (Herman 1992/2015,
p. 155). Consider how the structure of a Christian worship
service enacts and supports the post-traumatic journey:

Stage one of trauma recovery is safety and the integrity of
the body. In worship the congregation gathers together in what
is assumed to be and often experienced as a safe-enough place
and proceeds to seek to get right with neighbour and God
through confession and assurance of grace.

Stage two of trauma recovery majors on remembering and
mourning as part of the process of constructing a new story
that integrates the traumatizing event into the life of an individual and a community. In worship Word and Sacrament
are offered and explored to resource these activities, enabling
reflection on the traumatizing event within the larger story of
God and the people of God.

Stage three of trauma recovery is about reconnection and
re-entry into the community. In worship the prayers of inter-
cession turn the congregation's attention to the larger world
and in the dismissal it is charged with going out to love and to
serve.

Victor Turner (2008, p. vi), who spoke of ritual as 'the work
of the gods' channelling common energies and inculcating a
sense of moral purpose, extended van Gennep's analytical
structure with a particular focus on the second stage of transition and its characteristic of liminality. Liminality, from the
Latin *limen* meaning 'threshold', describes the state of being in
transition from one status or way of being to another. Liminal
spaces are inherently creative and capable of holding paradox
and strong emotion. They make a container for what needs to
happen for a person or community to move towards another
state of being. Prayer, ritual, music, art, play and poetry are
liminal activities. The heart of the worship service (stage two
in Herman's terms) is liminal space.

Recall the earlier discussion of lamentation in Chapter 10
with Brueggemann's characterization of psalms of lament as
facilitating movement between disorientation to new orientation. Traumatizing events are disorienting and disordering

and spark strong emotional reactions. Liminal spaces and practices like lamentation have the capacity to hold people as they grieve, wrestle chaos and prepare to pick up the pieces to adjust to a new normal that contains great loss. Well-crafted liturgy can be a safe container for the bedlam, strong emotion and imaginative possibility that will fuel movement through the threshold towards re-entry into the world.

We are instinctively drawn to perform rituals. Andrew Nunn, Dean of Southwark Cathedral, tells the story of a simple liturgy for moving the dead flowers and post-it notes from London Bridge in the aftermath of the 2017 terror attack. After a brief prayer acknowledging that each bloom represented life, the mayor and diverse clergy stepped forward to pick up a few bunches and move towards a van where council workers were ready to receive them and then collect the rest. What happened next was very moving: the crowd formed an orderly procession and silently moved forward to pick up bunches and place them in the van. It was a spontaneous people's liturgy.[1]

Liturgy also provides a language for suffering when trauma renders us speechless. Timeless and trustworthy, the words of the liturgy carry us through the roiling waters. The expectant silences cushion our sadness. The stories of our ancestors in faith – recorded in our robust, resilient scripture – reassure us that we are not alone and nourish our meaning-making. Ritual actions like baptism and communion weave us together with the communion of saints and inscribe the name *Beloved* on our consciousness. Our being and our becoming nurtured, come the end of the hour we may be ready to re-engage the world.

We not only stand before God in our times of worship; we stand with one another. Turner (2008, pp. 97, 126–9) emphasized the role of the community in ritual. We are witnessed. We are upheld in one another's presence. Human beings are profoundly relational. In the aftermath of a traumatizing event, we are consoled by the warm empathetic presence of another. It is the single most effective healing response to trauma. We are, as I have said before, made for love. It is love that liturgy, at its best, can channel to embrace broken hearts and disrupted nervous systems.

In the early hours after a shock event

In the immediate aftermath of a traumatizing event people need to gather and to acknowledge the horror of what has happened. Traumatizing events isolate. We are cut off from our resources and our assumptions about how the world and life should be are shattered. Gathering counteracts isolation and sends the implicit messages that we are in this together and that cooperation is possible. As noted in Part 1, churches have remarkable resources for gathering: physical premises that hold generations of prayer and hope, facilities for tea-making and rotas of volunteers, listening ears and serving hearts. Opening the church signals Christ's presence to hurting people and makes possible some of the other early interventions that will decrease suffering in the long run. Recall the Three C's: calm, communication, care. Early on gathering spaces and events are oases where information may be communicated and resonant care offered. The key element is warm presence. People simply need to be in a safe place together and to know that they are cared for.

Such spaces and events can include opportunities to engage with powerful liminal practices. Candle-lighting is an act both of defiance against the encroaching shadows and of hope. Memorial boards, books or notes place the names and prayers of the people before God and the community. Shared silences weave a bond of awed humility and unity while honouring diverse experiences. Singing together regulates breath and calms jangled nervous systems. Honesty and lamentation give voice to pain and terror and place the matter in the ambit of the Holy. This is all groundwork for the later, sometimes much later, work of meaning-making and repair.

If possible, collaboration with ecumenical or interfaith partners and local agencies can offer a broader scope for shared love and service and reinforce the message of human goodness and mutuality. Against the devastation wreaked by people or an unruly earth, a cooperative human response comforts the sorrowful and nurtures the possibility of new life in the days, weeks and months to come.

The first Sunday

John Swinton (2009, pp. 90–2) tells the story of going to church the Sunday after the 1998 Omagh bombing, shocked and hurting from the deaths of 28 people (including nine children) and the injuring and maiming of 220 more. Yet nothing was said, no prayer offered, no lamentation uttered. As he reflected on it he realized that his church had no capacity in its worship for dealing with sadness, brokenness or questioning. This was more than a missed opportunity. It revealed a contemporary disabling of the church to deal with real life.[2] The first Sunday after a traumatizing event must seek to meet people's needs in some way.

Every traumatizing event is unique. Tolstoy observed that all happy families are alike but each unhappy family is unhappy in its own way.[3] So it is with trauma. The nature and duration of the event, its impact on members of the community, the context and the available resources are just a few of the factors that will require prayerful consideration about how to proceed. The general principle is that the liturgy should neither avoid nor totally dwell on the tragedy. Bringing people's reality before God enables them to stand whole in themselves before the Holy. Emotions may be raw or strong so care must be taken about language and bounded space and time.

You may trust the liturgy to be the container for pain or confusion. The normal rhythm will be a stabilizing comfort. The movement of gathering, listening and responding carries the congregation on a journey of the soul that enables encounter with the Holy and the nourishment of Word and Sacrament. However, one of the challenges of Christian liturgy with its opening focus on the confession of sin is that it is more helpful for sinners than it is for those wounded by sin, which can reinforce disabling shame. While self-blame is an early coping mechanism and may or may not be appropriate as discussed elsewhere, perhaps the liturgy will need to be gently massaged to provide balm for wounds.

You may also be able to trust the lectionary. A priest was faced with preaching the Sunday after the suicide of a 14-year-old daughter of the church, only to discover that the lectionary included the story of Jesus raising to life a 12-year-old girl with the words *Talitha cum*. He wrestled mightily about whether to preach on it and in the end did:

> I said, 'this reading is probably the hardest we could have had for this Sunday'. I said there was going to be no *'talitha cum'*. There was going to be no 'get up, little girl'. And I said, 'I don't know how to deal with this'. I burst into tears. The whole church burst into tears. Everybody had gathered – like, what are we going to do in church today? How are we going to do church today? [pause] But, I think in that sense the reading was something of a gift. Because I think there was only one way to confront what had happened and that was head on. You know, warm words, hopefulness, it wasn't going to cut it. So I think that reading set for us, in a sense just made us as a church say it how it was ... then all these people just rushed up onto the stage and there was the whole church gathered in one place – like a huge group hug ... one thing I didn't want was ice cold professional. This was a real story and a real reaction, and anything other than a real service would have been a pseudo-thing, a fake, and as it happened, thanks to the reading, I was able to avoid faking it.[4]

The priest then reflected that the structure of the liturgy had made it safe to speak openly in the sermon. It was followed by reflective music based on Psalm 23; the intercessions allowed for privacy from the gaze of others and time for breath and earnest prayer. Nonetheless it must be observed that this would not have had the same outcome in every church. Knowing one's congregation and prayerful discernment will shape the choice of scripture.

The Eucharist or Holy Communion may be particularly helpful for some people, especially if it is the church's normal practice. The sacrament full of silence, movement and embodied activity (eating and drinking) in memory of the traumatizing event of Jesus' crucifixion can be a strong container for the wordless pain of trauma. The presence of Christ a companion in suffering, its medicine can be strong. For others, however, it may be problematic, with a potential to exacerbate vulnerability to harm, to retraumatize some survivors and to re-cast violence as positive or even necessary (Scarsella 2018, pp. 225–52; O'Donnell 2019, pp. 182–93).

After the first Sunday

In the aftermath of a traumatizing event, in general it is important to continue with normal events unless it is clear that it is not appropriate or not possible. The normal church diary can help structure people's time and stabilize their expectations. If it is not possible, other means may be found of keeping people connected to the faith community and the resources of faith. In the months of Covid-19 lockdown, churches with the ability to do so found purchase in technology and began to livestream worship, hold internet conferences for coffee hour, Bible study or prayer groups, and distribute Sunday services and newsletters electronically. Churches with older, less technologically agile or accessible congregations used telephone calls and the post.

Trauma cuts people off from their resources. Gathering weekly (or more often) within the congregation connects them to the community and the rich and deep resources of the faith: scripture, prayer, study, fellowship, acts of love and service. As the weeks and months go by, worship and small group gatherings enable people to heal and to make sense of what has happened. Broken relationships may be addressed through confession and reconciliation. Scripture and sermons fund the creation of a new narrative that is connected to the grand narrative of God's love and purposes and which includes and may even make sense of the traumatizing event. At the end of the service people are sent out to reconnect with the world, having drunk from the ever-flowing spring.

Worship during the disillusionment phase

The most difficult times in the life of the church are those when energy is low and despair high. The disillusionment phase in the journey of post-traumatic remaking is a time of wandering in the wilderness. It is a painful and chaotic period, difficult to traverse. The church facilitates forward movement by balancing respite and comfort with the hard work of facing into the difficulties. After the heroics of the early response to the traumatizing event, people need moments of peace and relaxation to regain their energy. Moments of levity and celebration may be a welcome opportunity to remember that life contains joy too. People also need encouragement and guidance to handle strong negative emotions and to address the true impact of what has happened. The leader's capacity to invite and welcome negative expression is essential so that people may rest as well as honestly rage, grieve and lament.

Recall from the chapter on lamentation Brueggemann's three urgent tasks in the face of a cataclysm: face reality, grieve, hope. Lamentation in the disillusionment phase fosters acceptance that what has happened has happened and that its impact is real. Recall that on the ICTG chart (Appendix C) the turn towards rebuilding and restoration happens when enough people can accept that and can also see the good in life.

The disillusionment phase is not a time to duck issues or sugar-coat life. Traumatizing events strip away illusions and unmask assumptions, driving some people to deep wrestling. As Jacob wrestled the stranger at the ford of the Jabbok until he was given a blessing, such wrestling can deepen faith. Ministers can give permission for hard questions and, after resonant caring, may be able to offer sustenance for the journey. Many and moving are the examples of those who walked this way before us in the Bible: Adam and Eve's exile from the garden; Hagar's banishment; Jacob's journey; the freed slaves' 40 years of wilderness wandering; Job's catastrophe; Jerusalem's destruction. In the aftermath of trauma these stories take on a new power and poignancy.

Preaching in the disillusionment phase may need to be more directive. The congregation needs guidance walking the treacherous way. As discussed in Chapter 9, issues of denial, the pressure to forgive or the blaming of victims will impede the journey. Grief needs to be facilitated to make way for acceptance and the turn towards hope. Real hope – not pie in the sky, everything will be OK hope, but the kind of hope that is resolute in believing that God is and that God will not let us go – needs to be nourished. And people need comfort. They are broken; they are tired.

Worship leadership in the disillusionment phase can be characterized as tough yet tender, reality-based and rooted-in-hope, honest and fearless and kind.

Worship in the rebuilding and restoration phase

Once enough people have accepted the reality of the traumatizing event and are healed enough to see that there is good in life as well as bad, the community begins to turn in fits and starts towards the work of rebuilding and restoration. Sparks of new initiatives that began to flare in the disillusionment phase may become warming flames. The congregation is still in transition but there is more positive energy alongside times of renewed pain and conflict. The spiritual work of lamentation has come to an end. Prayerful discernment about what the congregation needs continues. It is difficult to speak confidently about what should happen in this phase.

Speaking generally, sermons that indirectly address issues are better. The time for head-on confrontation and direction is gone. Instead, what is needed is the space for people to make meaning. Jesus told parables, allowing people to locate themselves in the story and take from it what they needed and what they were ready to hear. Wondering is good practice, in worship, Bible study or small groups. *I wonder where you have sensed God in these months. I wonder where God is leading us.* The process of rebuilding the shattered assumptions and constructing a new narrative robust enough to hold both pain and hope is a mysterious one. We will look more closely at it in Part 3.

Recall Layzell's wisdom (2019) from Chapter 9: once lamentation is neither necessary nor helpful, it is important to allow space and intentional silence in regular worship. One never knows what is being held or struggled with in the hearts gathered on a Sunday morning. In the quiet, people meet God as they are: wounded or wondering, hurting or hoping. And God meets them. This wise practice is born of the knowledge that life has trauma and suffering in it. *Come to me, all you that are weary and are carrying heavy burdens* (Matthew 11.28 NRSV).

Extraordinary services

While the regular diet of Sunday worship is a reliable vehicle for the journey of recovery, there are times and events that call for extraordinary worship services to aid movement forward. Rededications of sacred space, the remembrance of community tragedy, thanksgiving for first responders and other significant aspects provide opportunities for remembering or celebrating the congregation's life and journey. The potential power of anniversaries and commemorative objects will be discussed at the end of this section.

There are a number of things to consider in the planning of an extraordinary service. What follows is a list and brief description of them.

1 *Context*: Who is in the community (age/ethnicity/religion)? How has the traumatizing event impacted them? What are people thinking and feeling? What do they need? Who are the 'stakeholders' and how will they be consulted and co-opted?
2 *Purpose*: Who is the service for: the congregation, the wider community, the nation? Is the purpose remembrance, grief, thanksgiving?
3 *Timing*: Is now the right time? What is the sense of stakeholders (survivors, members of the community)?

4 *Location*: Where is the right place to hold it? How will the setting attract the intended congregation? Who will be less likely to attend because of the setting and how can that possible effect be mitigated?

5 *Language and silence*: What language can you borrow? Will it reflect the experience of the congregation and respect the setting? If the setting is interfaith or secular, will and how will Christian language be used authentically and sensitively? Will there be sufficient silence for people to attend to what is happening in them?

6 *Inclusion:* Who will you invite? Who will you include in the prayers? These questions can be tricky when traumatizing events have been caused or exacerbated by other people, as was the case in the 2017 Grenfell fire in London which will be discussed below, or when the victims include those who perpetrated violence.

7 *Non-verbal communication*: As much as the language used, the means of communication speaks loudly. A warm, sensitive presence that has obviously consulted widely will be trusted. Symbolic acts and activities that call for participation or movement also speak volumes.

8 *Room for flexibility?* Recall the earlier example given by Andrew Nunn with regard to the crowd's opportunity to create a people's liturgy to move dying flowers from London Bridge; it could have been nullified by an anxious leader's insistence on following the plan.

The outworking of these kinds of questions can be seen in the example of the Grenfell Tower National Memorial Service held in December 2017 in St Paul's Cathedral, London, six months after the fire that resulted in the death of 72 people. The service is discussed and reproduced in *Tragedies and Christian Congregations* (Grosch-Miller 2019c, pp. 155, 157–8, Appendix 6).[5] Conceived as a service of remembrance, community and hope and televised by the BBC, it was a moment for the nation to grieve and remember and for the survivors to feel held, their suffering acknowledged. The widespread appreciation for how it was structured and conducted reflected the months of careful listening and consultation that went into the service. Difficult issues of who should be invited – the council who had oversight of the cladding that appeared to cause the rapid spread of the fire? – and how to make the space and the liturgy truly welcoming for diverse communities were faced and wrestled. The timing of the service, asked for by survivor groups, was thought to be too early by some clergy, but in the end the mantra *the survivor is the expert* proved true. The use of voices and music from affected communities, the carrying of photographs of lost loved ones, the employment of the Grenfell green heart and white roses, and the use of silence all contributed to creating an extraordinary and meaningful event.

Ordinary services may include extraordinary liturgies to assist the journey of recovery. During the Covid-19 pandemic, author and liturgist Thom M. Shuman[6] wrote a 'World Communion Liturgy for a Time of Pandemic', for which he has generously agreed to grant permission to be reprinted as Appendix G.

Remembering: anniversaries, commemoration

The marking of horrific events provides opportunities for the essential work of grieving, remembering and integrating the tragedy into the story of a community or place. Anniversary services the first year after the event may be particularly meaningful and helpful. Kraus, Holyan and Wismer (2017, pp. 95–8) tell the story of the one-year anniversary marking of the murder of the sexton and a parishioner in the sanctuary of a church, a service that included the prayerful writing and burning of the congregation's hopes and fears. The liturgy was repeated in the second and third years, with a change of focus the third year away from the tragedy and towards the general hopes and fears of the congregation. In the fourth year no one asked to mark the anniversary. Once again, the survivors are expert – they know what they need.

Commemoration can happen in other ways: the creation of commemorative objects, the honouring of wounds. The considerations discussed above under 'Extraordinary services' again come into play. To be meaningful and effective, clarity about purpose and consultation with those most impacted by the tragedy are essential. A well-intended effort without such consultation may fall flat or, worse, offend. An outstanding example of the creation of meaningful commemorative objects is Southwark Cathedral's composting of the dying flowers collected off London Bridge and using them in a large planter holding a mature olive 'Tree of Healing'. Around the edge of the pot are inscribed: 'And the leaves of the tree are for the healing of the nations' (Grosch-Miller 2019c, pp. 162–4). Borough Market was uncomfortable with a permanent memorial to the attack in its grounds, fearing it would put visitors off. The cathedral churchyard is the home of the Tree, holding the community memory. The cathedral also chose to preserve the sacristy doors, scarred by police battering rods as they sought the perpetrators of the attack. As Jesus bore the wounds of crucifixion, so too the church bears the marks of violence from that day.

Key takeaway points

- Worship and liturgy are containers for the work of post-traumatic recovery throughout the long aftermath.
- Every traumatizing event is unique and calls for prayerful discernment of appropriate responses.
- In the early hours after a traumatizing event people need to gather in a safe space.
- The first Sunday after the event the tragedy should not be avoided nor should the service completely dwell on it.
- The liturgy and maybe the lectionary may be trusted.
- In the disillusionment phase worship can enable grief or rage through the practice of lamentation and sermons may be more directive. Difficult issues should be addressed.
- In the rebuilding and restoration phase sermons that address issues indirectly foster meaning-making as does the practice of wondering.

- Extraordinary services provide extraordinary opportunities to meet people and the community at a point of need. Consultation with those most impacted is essential.

Notes

1 The Very Revd Andrew Nunn, interview with Tragedy and Congregations team.

2 Southgate (2019b, p. 131) proposes that ministers enable broad exposure to the whole of scripture to build the congregation's capacity to respond helpfully to traumatizing events.

3 Leo Tolstoy, 1878, *Anna Karenina.*

4 The Revd Nick Bundock, interview with the Congregations and Tragedy team.

5 The appendices in Warner et al. 2019, *Tragedies and Christian Congregations*, provide liturgical material from the reopening of Southwark Cathedral after the 2017 terrorist attack at London Bridge and in Borough Market, and a cleansing celebration of the life of the city of Salisbury in 2018 after the Novichok nerve-agent poisonings. Also discussed in the liturgy chapter of the book are the first Sunday after the Grenfell fire in St Clement's Church; the Grand Iftar at Southwark Cathedral on the first anniversary of the Borough Market attack; an annual service for bereaved families at Aldgate Tube Station after the 2007 bombing; and the blessing or re-dedication of violated or damaged places (secular and sacred) in London, Somerset and Cumbria (Grosch-Miller 2019c).

6 Shuman is a contributor to Wild Goose publications and the author of *Where the Broken Gather: Lectionary Liturgies for RCL Year B*, 2014, and other books and liturgies posted online.

PART 3

The Changing Story of Life and Faith

Traumatizing events change a person and a community. In these chapters we consider how some of that change happens through the process of making meaning that is integral to recovery from trauma. Chapters 13 and 14 on meaning-making and on the God questions are more theoretical than those in Parts 1 and 2, but will equip you to recognize natural processes in survivors and to accompany and resource the journey of recovery. Chapter 15 reflects on recovery and resilience.

13

Finding Words:
Memory, Meaning-making
and Narrative

Trauma renders us speechless yet compels us (when we are ready) to speak of it. The shattering of our fundamental assumptions makes life incomprehensible, yet recovery demands that it be comprehended. It is through story that life is pieced together and made meaningful again.

We are story-making and storytelling beings. In both individuals and communities of faith, the story we tell about ourselves gives us an identity, structures our expectations and shapes our behaviours. Storytelling is probably a brain obsession, observes neuroscientist Antonio Damasio (2000, p. 89). One's story of one's self is built up over time, changing as new experiences are interpreted, synthesized and plotted to give life an intelligible shape. This happens mostly below the surface of consciousness. It is not a solo endeavour. The culture and people around us shape our story.

As discussed in Part 2, the capacity of the human being to function in the world – to plan and to act – is facilitated by a set of fundamental assumptions about the safety, benevolence, order and comprehensibility of the world, and about our own worthiness and adequacy. These assumptions are embedded, structural beliefs about the trustworthiness of the world, other people and ourselves. They are created out of our earliest experiences of life and through our relationships with our primary carers, fulfilling primary psychological needs for safety, trust/dependence, control, intimacy and esteem (Rando 2002, p. 179).

When a person or community is traumatized, one or more of those fundamental assumptions is shattered. The underpinning of the story of who we are is pulled out from under us. The world is no longer trustworthy. If the traumatizing event is caused by human action, people are no longer trustworthy. That such a thing, whatever it is, could happen to me suggests that I am not worthy.

In the crucible of a traumatizing event, our story is disrupted and meaning is upended and suspended. In the individual, efforts to grapple with what has happened are impeded by the fragmented nature of memory discussed in Part 1. Traumatic memories are a collection of sensory and emotional traces: pictures, sounds, and physical sensations with no organized, coherent story of what happened. In the community, diverse experiences of the traumatizing event further complicate the already complex task of assimilating the event into the collective story. In both, interpreting and integrating the event into the story of life is a primary task for recovery. This is an arduous and sometimes painful meaning-making, assumption-rebuilding endeavour.

Meaning-making and narrative in the individual

The reconstructed story must not only account for the experience, but also rebuild fundamental assumptions in a helpful way that will enable adequate functioning. In fact, it appears that it is the shattering of fundamental assumptions in the wake of the traumatizing event that sparks the meaning-making process (Park 2016, p. 1235).[1] The distress of the shattering triggers meaning-making methods, the results of which affirm or adapt the person's assumptions, beliefs, goals and values.

Methods of meaning-making include: 1) assimilation, whereby the traumatizing event is reinterpreted to better fit the individual's assumptions; 2) accommodation, which is a reconsideration and reshaping of assumptions; 3) unintentional processes such as intrusive thoughts or dreams which are automatic information processes; and 4) interactions with others (discussed briefly above in Chapter 9). The latter includes strategies of comparison with others who were more badly affected, self-blame and finding benefit and purpose in the event (Janoff-Bulman 1992, pp. 115, 125–30).

As regards fundamental assumptions, we prefer to assimilate the new situation if possible. We cling to our fundamental assumptions and, in our interpretations of what happened, seek to maximize the possibility of again apprehending the world, others and self as trustworthy, minimizing the difference between what we have experienced and the old assumptions. When that is not possible the old assumptions must be reformed. That is difficult and painful work that takes place in the face of psychological and cognitive-emotional disintegration (Janoff-Bulman 1992, pp. 90, 114).

While the cognitive aspects of meaning-making are important, fundamental assumptions are not primarily cognitive. Rather, the ways of living and being that we develop are products of interaction with 'noncognitive, emotional, psychological, physical, behavioural, social, soulful and spiritual forces and contexts' (Attig 2002, p. 60). Our ways-of-living assumptions function automatically and habitually without our thinking. When life is disrupted and these ways are no longer viable, there is much more going on than a conscious, cognitive re-shaping of the frameworks that support our living.

The experience of meaning-making is chaotic. It may begin before the nervous system is calmed and is enhanced when there is enough safety for the brain to function. Of necessity it is a slow and gradual activity. The work is never entirely complete as interpretations of the traumatizing event continue to re-form over time (Park 2016, p. 1239).

Meaning-making happens as stories are told and retold. By narrating events we assume control – turning from passive to active and exercising agency. Naming creates new neural pathways and integrates the feeling and thinking brain (recall Chapter 2). Storytelling is an act of agency that reclaims the sense of personal worthiness and adequacy that has been shattered by the traumatizing event. The starting point appears to be creating a basic narrative which begins to answer the question *Why did this happen?*, thereby achieving a cognitive mastery that is foundational to coping and adjustment. We have all heard and perhaps said *Why me?* in the wake of unwelcome events. While answering the causal questions for oneself is not sufficient for recovery, it is necessary for the restoration of a sense of safety and control.

The stories we tell are told to others. Their witnessing presence is powerful. As discussed in Part 1, the strongest predictor of recovery and minimized distress for a traumatized individual is the presence of another person who is a warm, empathetic accompanier. As we speak of what has happened and are received, we learn to bear the wound and to connect our inner and outer reality. It is an inherently integrative process. The others to whom we tell the story hold our social context and cultural expectations and behaviours, and so shape the process and outcome of rebuilding assumptions. For whom we tell the story is an important shaper of the story that cannot be overestimated (Ganzevoort 1998, p. 278).

Story-making and telling is a creative activity, calling on the imagination. Serene Jones (2009, p. 20) speaks of the work of trauma recovery as a healing of imagination that enables us to again tell stories' about ourselves and the world that are life-giving. We are restored not just into being able to function in our everyday world, but into the possibility of a future that contains hope.

An aside: I know something about this type of journey. From January 2014 through Easter 2016, I lived through a cascade of family deaths, beginning with the violent sudden death of my brother, while coping with an assumption-shattering ministry situation. By Easter I was on my knees and on my way out of ministry. What followed was an extraordinary few years which began with me being unable to bear church, having become deeply disillusioned about the possibility of God. I let go of the idea of faith and God, desiring desperately to know what was Real. Slowly, slowly as I clung fiercely to my desire for reality, things began to shift within me – I cannot tell you how. I was writing poetry to save my life (which became *Lifelines: Wrestling the Word, Gathering Up Grace*, 2020). I was learning to care for body, mind and soul. We relocated to the north-east of England and opportunities arose that enabled my healing mind to process what had happened to me as I learned about and taught trauma. I assessed and reassessed the church-related trauma. I learned to bear the wound of death. If I had to sum up the journey, I would say it was a great letting go, a letting be and an opening. I am both the same and a different person now: more capable of self-care and able to trust inner wisdom; more slow-moving; deeply respectful of the integrity of individual journeys; quietly trusting in the mysterious ways of grace; brave (I hope) about what is Real, which includes God, the source of being and becoming. I am humble before the terror of our vulnerability and humanity's foibles and failures, including my own. It was as I wrote the introduction to *Lifelines* at Easter 2019 that I was able to look back and see the journey as a form of death and resurrection. That is my story.

Not all rebuilt assumptions and not all stories lead to life. Sometimes assumptions are changed to make the world feel less safe and stories are told that foster harm. Prejudice can be buttressed. Individual flourishing can be impeded by fear and vigilance. Particularly, blaming others is found to lead to poorer outcomes,[2] as is the conclusion that one is being punished by God (Park 2016, p. 1239). When considering meaning-making, it is also important to consider *what* meaning is made and whether and how that contributes to the individual's well-being.

Narrative and community recovery

Collective trauma requires collective responses. Particularly in historically significant events, constructing a collective story is critical to giving the shared experience of trauma meaning and purpose.

Every collective trauma is unique unto itself. The nature, severity and impact of the traumatizing event, the context and the resources of the community will differ in each case.

The post-traumatic journey to recovery will be shaped by the culture of the community. That is why Saul's Community Resilience Model of trauma recovery (2014) includes broad-based collective storytelling that reflects diverse experiences and community healing rituals, as described in Part 2.

Yet not every community and not every trauma lends itself to communal storytelling. Some traumatizing events, such as clergy sexual abuse, are so shaming and divisive that a pall of silence falls over the congregation. This is contributed to by the limited amount of information that is available to the congregation for a long time when a minister is under investigation or subject to disciplinary or legal proceedings. And some congregations are simply wary of confronting difficult questions that may impact their sense of cohesion, preferring to pour oil on turbulent waters.

There also may be at work the complex phenomenon of denial among some of the individuals in a traumatized community. Denial is a means of managing anxiety that threatens to be overwhelming (Parkes 2002, p. 240). It is a common response in the early aftermath of a traumatizing event (Janoff-Bulman 1992, p. 101). Sometimes denial is adaptive, giving people a chance to recoup energy. Recall the oscillation of avoidance and intrusive memory of early coping described in Part 2. In such cases denial is postponement. But denial may be maladaptive if it persists, preventing the kinds of collective mourning and storytelling that enable post-traumatic recovery and re-making.

Still other phenomena contribute to vast silences in the wake of a cataclysmic event. The shattering and loss of an assumptive world with its accompanying powerlessness can manifest in shame (Kauffman 2002, p. 206). The magnitude of suffering may be such that its incomprehensibility prevents coherent speech. It took several years for survivors of the Holocaust to speak of it (Krystal 2002, p. 214).[3] Many of us will know of grandparents or great-grandparents who did not speak of their war experiences until late in their lives, decades later. Cultural values may stifle speech, generally (stiff upper lip, keep calm and carry on) or through the marginalization of subgroups in the community. And there is the danger that speaking of atrocity may be retraumatizing (van der Kolk 2014, p. 204).

There is a time lag between experiencing a traumatic event and being able to work with it. The passage of time permits traumatizing events to be confronted at a safe distance (Frechette and Boase 2016, p. 12). Different representational forms provide distance and spark the imagination to make meaning of what has happened: poetry, music, art, bodily movement, religious ritual, literary construction (Frechette and Boase 2016, pp. 6–7). As discussed in Chapter 12, the worship life of a faith community can hold, resource and bless the reframing that participants do as together the people read the Word, share the bread and the wine, and re-member God's redeeming work.

Our Bible gives a powerful witness to the traumatic process through literature. The story of the siege and fall of Jerusalem and the carrying off of people into exile is told briefly and summarily in 2 Kings 24 and 25. But the impact of those events on the collecting, rewriting and redacting of the stories of the ancestors in the aftermath was profound, as explored in Chapter 11. The stories of Abraham and Moses were refigured to heal the memory of devastation and exile (Carr 2014, pp. 101–16). New texts were written: Jeremiah's pain in poetry and prose testifies to survival (Stulman 2016, pp. 125–39). Deutero-Isaiah (40—55) brought messages of comfort, revenge and renewal to the exiles (Frechette 2016, pp. 67–83). The book of Ezekiel rewrites history to place the contemporary cataclysm in a context of cause and effect, offering a possibility for comprehending the incomprehensible (Poser 2016, p. 33). Lamentations articulates the pain of that destruction, moving 'from the fragmentation and isolation of individual suffering to the formation of a new communal identity', unifying and reforming the community as it makes new meaning from the ruins (Boase 2016, p. 62). This is the power of collective meaning-making writ large.

In *Tragedy and Christian Congregations*, I tell the story of a church which experienced the suicide of a teenage girl. The church had their world rocked when the coroner announced, months later, that it appeared that the young woman had killed herself because she thought she was unacceptable to God, her church and her family because of her sexuality. The bombshell of this announcement sparked a long personal and communal process of re-evaluating their theology of same-sex relationships that was often arduous and painful. I identify in that chapter what assists the hard work of both personal and collective meaning-making: facing into the traumatizing event and acknowledging its pain and disorienting impact; providing a container for strong emotion; resourcing the cognitive work that needs to be done; and journeying together (Grosch-Miller 2019a, pp. 28–40).

Accompanying those who seek to make meaning from the terrible thing they have survived can be arduous. Perhaps the most important thing to remember is that it is *their* task. We are to hold the space open with resonant care and sensitively to offer resources. The meaning they come to may not be the meaning we would make. The survivor is the expert in their recovery. In the next chapter we consider the God questions, an important part of meaning-making for the Christian.

Key takeaway points

- Personal and communal identity is constructed and re-modelled through story-making and storytelling.
- Traumatizing events shatter fundamental assumptions about the trustworthiness of the world, other people and the self, disrupting the life story and sparking meaning-making processes.
- Interpreting and integrating the traumatizing event into the life story is a primary task for recovery.
- Meaning-making is a complex cognitive and emotional, conscious and non-conscious process that is gradual, slow and painful. It is ongoing.
- A witnessing presence is an important part of storytelling.
- Poetry, art, music, movement, ritual and literary construction are means of making shared meaning in a community.

- The Bible provides a powerful witness of the communal traumatic recovery process.
- Communal meaning-making is assisted by facing fully into the traumatizing event, providing a container for strong emotion, resourcing the cognitive work that needs to be done, and intentionally journeying together.

Notes

1 Crystal Park (2016, p. 1235) absorbs fundamental assumptions into 'global meaning' which includes one's sense of meaning and purpose, goals and values.

2 Blaming the perpetrator, rather than self-blame, is helpful and related to better outcomes for survivors of incest.

3 The wounding was so shattering that there were no contemporaneous witnesses speaking of it during the Holocaust. Elie Wiesel did not publish *Night* until 1960.

14

Imagining God

For my thoughts are not your thoughts, nor are your ways my ways, says the LORD. (Isaiah 55.8 NRSV)

The God questions: theodicy

At some point in the aftermath of a traumatizing event, God questions may arise. These are questions of ultimacy grounded in lived experience. They are part of the sense- and meaning-making that are necessary to post-traumatic remaking as we rebuild shattered assumptions and create a new narrative that integrates the unimaginable events into our life story and the larger story of the human family. This chapter seeks to offer theological frameworks, ideas and practices that may help you to accompany those who ask these kinds of questions.

Early on the questions come from a traumatized nervous system. The limbic system, you will recall from Chapter 1, is always asking *Am I safe? Do I belong?* The experience of trauma shatters thoughts of basic safety arising from the assumed benevolence of an ordered world and personal worthiness. R. Ruard Ganzevoort (2009, pp. 188–9) has translated these assumptions into theological language: that God is sovereign over an ordered world; that God can be trusted to be benevolent; and that God loves me. When the unexpected unimaginable happens, the world is revealed to be disordered or malevolent and our own lives to be far more vulnerable than we have allowed ourselves to know. If God is sovereign, why does God allow such harm and suffering? Is God trustworthy? Is God powerful and what is the nature of that power? If God is loving, am I unlovable? Is this my fault? Am I somehow to blame?

Theodicy is the Christian exploration that seeks to explain why a powerful, good and loving God created a world that contains moral and natural evil or suffering. Ganzevoort observes that various types of theodicies are evoked to cushion the shattering of assumptions.[1] While primarily an intellectual exercise, theodicies are also coping strategies addressed to limbic system distress. Diverse Christian understandings offer different theodical hypotheses. Punishment theodicies conclude that the person did something wrong or bad and now must suffer the consequences. The power of both God and the individual are preserved; divine and human agency intact, the person can continue to assume that they have control in future situations.[2] Educative theodicies present suffering as the way our souls are made, freedom being necessary in order for humans to learn to recognize and choose the good. Both punishment and educative theodicies downplay the severity or injustice of some suffering. They may be employed as intellectual defence mechanisms to block emotional distress and conflict (Swinton 2009, p. 12n3). They may also be meaningful, as the sufferer seeks to understand if their actions have caused the suffering and what lessons can be learned.

Comfort and solidarity theodicies posit the nearness of God as comfort, setting aside the why questions and drawing on the strength of Jesus's struggle against evil on the cross. Distance and mystery theodicies enter the dark night of the soul with its sense of abandonment and isolation, mirroring the cry of Psalm 22 from the cross, accepting that there may be no answers at least in the short term, and living into and through the pain of dislocation. There are other theodicies, some of which like process theology propose that God cannot intervene, having surrendered the power to coerce human beings and retaining only the power to persuade. In the chaos and pain of the aftermath of trauma, a person may move from one to another theodicy as they struggle to make sense of what has happened.

What is the role of the compassionate pastoral carer who is bombarded with God questions? It is not to give firm answers but to accompany the sense-making journey lightly, holding open the space to wonder and offering resources that may fit with where the sufferer is as they wrestle to find their way to firm ground on which they can stand.

Practical theodicy

John Swinton (2009, p. 13) warns that some theodicies may become a source of evil itself: '... in reality, we can never know the answers to the questions that so deeply trouble us. Indeed, attempting to know the unknowable can actually create fresh suffering and evil.' When a theodicy justifies and rationalizes evil, silences or unjustly blames the sufferer, or blocks people's access to the love and hope of God, it contributes to evil. Swinton (p. 30) holds the why questions of theodicy in tension with the question 'What does evil do?' and proposes a practical theodicy. Practical theodicy is

> the process wherein the church community, in and through its practices, offers subversive modes of resistance to the evil and suffering experienced by the world. The goal of practical theodicy is, by practicing these gestures of redemption, to enable people to continue to love God in the face of evil and suffering and in so doing to prevent tragic suffering from becoming evil. (Swinton 2009, p. 85)

He goes on to name those practices of redemption as lamentation, unforced forgiveness, thoughtfulness and hospitality.

Like Swinton, Ryan Patrick McLaughlin (2020, p. 10) believes that lamentation and protest are appropriate faith responses to the existence of evil and suffering. He argues that traditional theodicy should be held in irresolvable tension with an 'anti-theodicy' and the ethical response of protest, a 'sacramental moment of eschatological hope'. Anti-theodicy refuses to justify or explain God's responsibility, by design or by default, for suffering. Instead the focus is on right human response. McLaughlin (p. 10) quotes Elie Wiesel: 'It is given to [humanity] to transform divine injustice into human justice and compassion.'[3]

Faced with unthinkable suffering, the gut clenches and a fist is raised to the sky in protest. Then the community gets to work to meet real human needs.

As we shall see, practical and protest theodicies share with trauma theologies a serious engagement with lived human experience.

The theology of trauma

In the seventeenth century, Sir Francis Bacon observed that God was revealed in the Word and in the God-created world. While he cautioned about mingling these two unwisely, I think both are necessary. They are in essence all we have to seek to know the power that holds the universe together and incites life and love. Godself is beyond our limited understanding. Theology, like theodicy, is ultimately an act of the imagination, of seeking to know what is unknowable in its fullness.

Drawing on the sources of faith – scripture, tradition, reason and experience – theologians construct systems of meaning shaped by their understanding of the nature of those sources. Traditionally, scripture has been understood to be the primary source of authority as the Spirit-breathed revelation of the one, holy God. Christian tradition can be understood to be an outgrowth of scripture, developing dynamically in relationship to context and culture. Reason is both the application of logical method and the content of other bodies of non-theological knowledge, concerning which theologians have varying degrees of evaluation and acceptance. Experience has been treated with the most suspicion, being inherently subjective. Yet, as I argue in *Tragedies and Christian Congregations*, it has been the silent partner to the other sources (Grosch-Miller 2019a, pp. 29–31).

The most salient feature of trauma theologies is that they take the embodied, lived experience of human beings seriously. As such, trauma theologies naturally fall within practical theology, reflecting that discipline's commitment to exploring lived experience in conversation with theological and other sources and to seeking to craft faithful responses.

The powerful embodied impact of trauma requires that theology attend to lived experience in seeking to understand the traumatized human or community before and in God. But more than that, the lens of trauma enables theologians to mine Scripture and tradition for new insights that enrich the tradition. Shelly Rambo (2010) explores Holy Saturday to wrestle with the presence of death in life after trauma, expositing the presence of a middle spirit of weary love that is able to track the grief and loss while sensing the possibility of future life. In a later book she meditates on the presence of wounds in the risen body of Christ and Thomas' reaching out to touch them. Holding Scripture and trauma theory in creative conversation, she claims the power of wounds, surfaced and taken seriously, to form and transform the community to break the cycle of traumatic violence (Rambo 2017). Drawing on rich tradition – the reflections of Hans Urs von Balthazar and Adrienne von Speyr in *Spirit and Trauma* (Rambo 2010) and the scar of Macrina, sister of Gregory Nyssa, in *Resurrecting Wounds* (Rambo 2017) – Rambo breathes new life into the journey from Good Friday to Easter and maps the way the sacred story opens new possibilities for redeemed and resurrected life.

In trauma theologies new insights from Scripture and tradition are crafted in conversation that is both critical and liminal. Sometimes a doctrine or traditional understanding needs first to be deconstructed because of its impact on the lives of real human beings. Some of those impacts are traumatizing. As trauma shatters assumptions and shifts paradigms, so too it may foster shifts in Christian understanding and practice. Here the insights of Walter Brueggemann in *Reality, Grief, Hope* (2014) offer a framework for understanding the process.

As discussed above in Chapter 10 on lamentation, Brueggemann looks back at the events of the sixth century BC – the destruction of Jerusalem and the Temple, the exile to Babylon, and the drawn-out return to rebuild. He identifies the prophetic tasks[4] in the aftermath of a cataclysm as being to take reality seriously, to name and grieve the losses, and to nurture hope. The naming and grieving of losses assures that the impact of events is fully acknowledged.

The work of trauma theologians follows this framework. The O'Donnell and Cross (2020) collection of essays on feminist trauma theology name and take seriously the 'scar across humanity'[5] that is violence against women. Chapter after chapter names and examines the experience of trauma, some of it caused by Christian doctrine and practice. Scripture and doctrine are drawn out, sometimes critiqued, mined and put in service of reimagining a theology that 'does justice to the lives of real people' (O'Donnell and Cross 2020, p. xx). The writers are naming and grieving the losses – of life, of agency, of possibility – and they are nurturing hope by seeking to 'imagine what life-giving faith can be in today's world … attempting to build a viable structure … an inhabitable, beautiful, fruitful theology' (O'Donnell 2020, p. 1).[6] O'Donnell and Cross call these efforts constructive theology, recognizing that all theology is an imaginative endeavour to name the ultimately unknowable. Like practical theology, it takes human experience seriously and engages in interdisciplinary dialogue while mining Christian tradition.

O'Donnell (2020, pp. 13–14) highlights five aspects of feminist trauma theologies: 1) they begin from a place of honest confrontation with God; 2) they are 'porous' and open theologies that 'hold to the goods of Christian tradition while allowing space for something new to be spoken'; 3) they draw on experience, constructing narratives that testify; 4) they defy convention and seek to disrupt the established order that enables the oppression of women; and 5) they are community endeavours, 'standing shoulder to shoulder at the foot of the cross' like the Marys. From these she extrapolates a three-fold methodology that begins with a thick description of lived experience, moves to critical reflection on experience and on how it is perceived and treated in culture and Christian tradition, and develops as a community building project.

Implicit in this description is the imaginative nature of trauma theology. Not only does trauma theology dare to enter into the imaginative space of being traumatized, it also dares to imagine new ways of thinking about God and the divine–human relationship. It is to theology and the imagination that I now turn.

Imagining God anew: trauma and theological innovation

The biblical witness is that people have reimagined God when their experience has required it. When the dwelling place of God was destroyed and people were carried off into exile, the understanding that YHWH God was tied to a particular piece of land was no longer adequate. As discussed in Chapter 11, monotheism, one God universal over all the cosmos, took hold. Understandings of covenant, of punishment and of forgiveness evolved over time in response to wrestling with lived experience.

Trauma shatters assumptions and fosters paradigm shifts. The middle spirit that Rambo identifies as being present in the aftermath of trauma bears the seeds of a new day with a new way of thinking and being. Serene Jones (2009, p. 20) describes the work of recovery from trauma as a healing of the imagination. She explains:

I use the word [imagination] to refer to the fact that as human beings we constantly engage the world through organizing stories or habits of mind which structure our thoughts. Our imagination simply refers to the thought stories that we live with and through which we interpret the world surrounding us.

A traumatic event reconfigures the imagination, affecting our ability to tell stories about ourselves and our world that are life giving and lead to our flourishing.

Engagement with trauma caused a subtle and significant shift of consciousness about the theology of sin and grace in Jones. She observes that grace reshapes and enlarges our imagination, and that theology is 'the language that both describes the power and evokes it in the lives of people by telling grace-filled stories of new imaginings' (Jones 2009, pp. 21, 122–3). She identifies two transformative habits of spirit – mourning and wonder:

If imagination is comprised as much of flesh and heart as it is of beliefs and well-formed ideas, then it follows that these practices [mourning and wonder] eventually shifted my conscious theology of sin and grace. Not surprisingly, the change came without much fanfare, stopping short of a full-fledged conversion. It was significantly soul shifting, nonetheless, because it cultivated in me two forms of feeling-thought or, better, two habits of spirit that, when consciously accepted, rearranged my world ... Mourning fully and wondering openly – at the end of this book, this is what remains: the soul-response evoked by the cross. To mourn and to wonder, that is what the spirit yearns for when it stands in the midst of trauma and breathes in the truth of grace. Mourning and wonder – neither one answers the question that trauma poses to grace. They are, instead, states of mind that, if nurtured, open us to the experience of God's coming into torn flesh, and to love's arrival amid violent ruptures. (Jones 2009, p. 161)

Again Brueggemann's framework proves robust: bear reality, mourn and hope. Hope is the seedbed of imagination, the will to dare to contemplate that things can be different and better ... and that life will rise again. At the heart of imagining God is the conviction that love will find a way.

Key takeaway points

- Traumatic experiences generate God questions.
- A person may shift from one theodicy to another as they seek to find firm ground upon which to stand.
- The role of the pastoral carer is to accompany and resource the journey.
- Theodicy may best be held in tension with 'anti-theodicy', protest and lamentation.
- Trauma theologies engage with lived human experience and are practically oriented.
- Constructive theologies facilitate critiquing and developing theological understandings.
- Trauma can cause paradigm shifts and spark theological innovation.

Notes

1 R. Ruard Ganzevoort, conversation with the Congregational Trauma team.

2 The phenomenon of self-blame as an individual coping process is discussed in Chapter 9 (Picking up the Pieces) and as a communal response in Chapter 11 (The Bible).

3 Elie Wiesel, 1976, *Messengers of God*, trans. Marion Wiesel, New York: Random House.

4 And I would include the priestly and pastoral tasks.

5 Elaine Storkey, 2015, in *Scars Across Humanity: Understanding and Overcoming Violence Against Women*, London: SPCK, explores the violence against women that mars the entire globe.

6 O'Donnell (2020, p. 1) is quoting Paul Lakefield and Serene Jones (eds), 2005, *Constructive Theology: A Contemporary Approach to Classical Themes*, Minneapolis, MN: Fortress Press.

15

Recovery and Resilience

We find our way. Our way may not look exactly like anyone else's way. And after trauma we emerge changed – perhaps wiser and more resilient, perhaps (like Jacob) with a limp.

This chapter is a reflection on recovery and resilience during and after a terrible event or series of events happens, and a gathering up of strategies derived from recent research. Resilience is variously defined but in essence it is about surviving and coming back from adversity. It is a process and a product. It is something we can learn rather than purely an inborn trait. It is the way we recover and potentially become stronger.

Throughout there will be references to what has been explored in previous chapters, but there are two concepts that particularly form my thinking about resilience. The first is the trauma recovery mantra *the survivor is the expert*. The significance of this is that it requires careful listening to the survivor and respect for their autonomy and agency. One survivor's recovery journey and resilience strategies may not look like those of another. Will the survivor have all the answers all of the time? No. We all need support, encouragement and the resources that others can signpost. But the survivor will know what is right for them – what kind of support and encouragement and which resources will suit.

The second concept is that there is a shape to the journey, a shape like that of the 'Phases of Collective Trauma Response' chart in Chapter 8. That chart seeks to map out the journey for a community but many who look at it recognize their personal journeys of bereavement or trauma recovery. That shape is also revealed in the content of the book of Psalms which resources the human journey from orientation to disorientation and towards new orientation (Chapter 10), a journey we take over and over throughout our lives. The journey is long – two to five years after a single-event trauma. Having the patience to put one foot in front of the other is key. And just as different seasons require different clothing, the different phases require different energies and strategies.

I will address personal recovery and resilience before looking at communal or congregational resilience. The two, of course, are interrelated. A community is made up of individuals; their recovery journeys impact the communal journey and vice versa.

The heart of the matter: self-compassion

After two years of cascading family bereavements and professional challenges, the bottom of my world fell out and I was pressed down to the ground. My body and soul felt broken. All my natural effusiveness and compassion had died. Basic assumptions about life and God and myself were shattered. I could not look people in the eye. I could not bear to hear 'the promises of God' which had become as clanging cymbals to me.

What I most needed was rest and respite from trying to function as a minister and from having to relate to other human beings. Deep down I knew this. Not everyone agreed with me. I had functioned so well under stress for so long that people thought I could and should continue.

At the heart of recovery and resilience is deep listening for the compassionate inner voice that seeks to love us into life. It may sound like our own voice or like the sound of sheer silence. It is often drowned out by our own preconceptions and the expectations of others. But it is there ... whispering in the tissues of our bodies, echoing in the chambers of our gut. It is the song the dove sang as Jesus emerged from the Jordan. It is the golden thread that connects us to the Love that holds the cosmos together.

Self-compassion has become a lodestone for me. These naturally magnetic stones were the first compasses and featured in early navigation. In Middle English, *lodestone* meant 'course stone' or 'leading stone'. They are strong. They are trustworthy. They lead the way in every season.

Self-compassion is the key to resilience (Parry 2017a, p. 154):[1] it involves noticing what is happening inside and around you with kindness, not judging or evaluating, and responding to yourself as you would to your best friend. Recall the felt sense exercise in Chapter 2. Now imagine noticing the stress or sadness in your body and saying, *Oh darling, what do you need? Shall I make you a cup of tea?*

You may recoil at that kind of self-talk; that's OK. But any way that you can respond to yourself with gentleness and kindness opens the space for self-compassion to work its healing. Some of us have strong self-critics. We are more likely to berate, chastise, admonish and beat ourselves up than to ask ourselves kindly about what we need. We got this voice from somewhere, and it is likely that it has helped us to achieve things. But it can also harm us and get in the way of hearing and responding to what we really need. I recently heard Sharon Salzberg (2020) speak about her self-critic, who she calls Lucy (from the Charlie Brown comic). When Lucy pipes up, she simply notices, says *Hello* and then she may say something like *Chill out*. Sometimes she'll offer Lucy a cup of tea, but she won't let her run riot in the house. Even our self-critics are worthy of compassion (Tallentire 2017, pp. 46–59). They have wanted the best for us and worked hard to keep us safe and colouring within the lines. But they do not have to be in charge. Likewise, some of the coping strategies we have learned over the years may have defended and saved us in those moments but they may not serve us well in the long run.[2] The lodestone question when encountering our self-critic or when thinking about what we want and need is: *Is it helping me or harming me?* (Holland 2020a).[3] *What do I need?*

Finding the way

You will discover what works best for you. Only you will know what you need to come back to life. I needed to live in my body – to move and walk and swim and sing. I needed to be free of the expectations of others. I needed to be with people I love and who loved me, people with whom I could laugh and play and learn new things, people who just accepted me as I was. And what I wanted most was to know what was Real. What I could trust and rely on.

In and through the body: agency, rest, movement

Restoring agency is a crucial goal of trauma recovery, enabling the undoing and unlearning of helplessness that trauma inflicts. This is one of the reasons why the survivor is the expert. Only you know what works for you given your resources, life history and limitations. Doing something (anything) releases agency hormones that metabolize stress hormones. Agency – choosing, acting, participating – is correlated with resilience (Rolbiecki et al. 2017, pp. 89–94).[4] And it is intimately connected with our bodies. It begins with our awareness of subtle body-based feelings. The more aware we are of what is going on within us, the more we are able to have some control in our lives (van der Kolk 2014, p. 95). As we hone our ability for compassionate listening, we can trust our bodies to tell us what we need.

We need to act and we need to rest. Research confirms it: human beings, and especially people who have been traumatized, need rest (Nagoski and Nagoski 2019, pp. 154–87).[5] The experience of trauma and the journey in its aftermath is exhausting, particularly in the early stages. Rest is healing. Rest re-creates us. Rest makes us stronger. Sleep deprivation compromises physical and mental health. We are at our best in bursts, oscillating between work and rest. The standard expectation that ministry is a six-day-a-week role, often requiring long hours into the evening, is death-dealing. After decades of that routine my brain could no longer function without significant rest and re-creation. Years later it still cannot. Why do we expect ourselves or others to work long hours?

Rest is not just physical. Mental rest is as important: stepping away from tasks often brings new insights. Our brains need time to process what is happening internally and externally. Play too is re-creating rest. Play is how human beings create and discover ourselves (Winnicott 1971/2005, p. 73).

And we need to connect to our bodies, to move (Nagoski and Nagoski 2019, p. 15). Movement enables our bodies to metabolize the stress hormones that have been wreaking havoc on our organs and tissues, completing the stress cycle. Even the gentlest of walks connects us to ourselves and our environments and lets us know we are safe. When we move, we are fully alive.

Connection

People: can't live with them (sometimes), can't live without them (always). Other human beings can be a huge source of stress and distress, even and perhaps especially those we love, who may annoy, betray, or up and die on us. Yet we are made for connection with people. Connection with other human beings is a 'basic, biological need':

> Connection nourishes us in a literal, physiological way, regulating our heart rates and respiration rates, influencing the emotional activation in our brains, shifting our immune response to injuries and wounds, changing our exposure to stressors, and modulating our stress response. We literally sicken and die without connection. (Nagoski and Nagoski 2019, p. 134)

We need agency and autonomy – to be an 'I' – and we need connection and belonging – to be part of a 'we'.[6] We oscillate from one to the other, each of us finding the balance that best suits us. That balance is called 'self-differentiation'. Our whole lives we wrestle with these needs that are both complementary and competing. No person is an island (though sometimes we would like to live on a deserted one); we are created by relationship and community. The recovery and resilience journey may take us to a new place on the self-differentiation scale, for a short time or for ever. Self-differentiation, being an 'I' that belongs to a 'we', and boundaries enable us to know where we end and another person begins, so that we are not completely absorbed by the being or pain of another. These too contribute to resilience (Dekel 2017, pp. 10–17).

Every piece of research I have read on resilience has emphasized the role of social support or relationships (Holland 2020b).[7] From the time we are infants, we need other people to survive, grow and thrive.[8] Resonant care is the most powerful healer in the aftermath of trauma. In mutually supportive, honest relationships in which we are received as we are (with our vulnerabilities and our strengths), we learn to trust not only ourselves but other people. And others may model resilience which we pick up vicariously (Parry 2017b, p. 17). In the mirror of caring relationships, we experience our own worthiness and are strengthened to face into the winds of change and loss. We grow in courage.

The physicality of relationship matters too. Hugs that are wanted release endorphins – the feel-good hormones that defend against emotional distress (Jackson 2017, p. 26).[9] A twenty-second hug with someone you love and trust lowers blood pressure and heart rate, improves mood and impacts hormones, so that after a hug levels of oxytocin (social bonding) rise (Nagoski and Nagoski 2019, pp. 16–17). It is no surprise that the loss of opportunities to touch during the Covid pandemic contributed significantly to people's suffering. Hugs, laughter, tears … all of these embodied expressions of trust and relationship heal and strengthen.

Meaning and purpose

Our need for belonging has a broader horizon. We need to belong to a larger purpose. We need a reason to live and a framework that makes sense of all that has happened. We need a sense that our life matters. These are the functions that meaning fulfils.

When we are traumatized our fundamental assumptions are torn asunder and the ground falls from beneath our feet. Our sense of self shatters and we are left scarcely able to pick up the pieces. Slowly, slowly, we gain strength and begin to rebuild. We may find the old framework sturdy enough to incorporate the fact that terrible things can and did happen (those frameworks are resilient). Or we may find the old framework is not sufficient. Looking for the Real, for ground on which we can stand, we piece together a new scaffolding which may contain substantial pieces of the old one and eventually supports the telling of a new story.

In earlier chapters I identified reframing – retelling the story of our life – as a strong resource in trauma recovery, one evidenced in our sacred scriptures. This meaning-making tool has been identified as important in resilience. As we rewrite the story focusing on how we survived (Nagoski and Nagoski 2019, pp. 69–70), we discover our strengths and the resources that enabled us to cope and grow. We learn that we can confront terrible things and survive and that resilience is both the process and the outcome.

Here is something very interesting: the greater our trauma, the more likely that we will experience significant post-traumatic growth (Nagoski and Nagoski 2019, p. 68).[10] The struggle can make us stronger. The truth is that becoming fully human is a struggle. Ask Jacob on the banks of the Jabbok. We learn more from failure than from success. Anything that is effortful for us makes an impression.

A corollary to this is that self-compassion is not fluffy blankets and bubble baths (although for some those can play a part). It is an open-hearted, eyes-wide-open stance towards ourselves that makes it possible to grapple with our weaknesses and vulnerabilities, even and especially those that may have contributed to the terrible thing. Once there has been enough distance and healing, adversity is our greatest teacher. We are exposed to the Real in ourselves and in the world. Sometimes it is not a pretty picture.

Self-compassion helps us to lean in with love to start to sort it out. We learn who we are and what we need. We discover that, like all humans, we are imperfect (Wilson 2017, pp. 32–45). We realize what happens when we don't attend to our needs, that we can become a danger to others. We take responsibility for our actions and for our growth. It is self-compassion that gives us a foundation of safety that allows us to embrace rather than avoid the pain of it all (Lawson 2017, pp. 115–16).

The struggle to become, to grow in maturity, is part of finding meaning and purpose in our lives and connecting to the wider world. In her study of the role of adversity in healing and growth, Justine Allain-Chapman identifies struggle to be in the essence of resilience building. She draws on the work of psychiatrist Frederic Fach and writes:

> Struggle arises because of the emotional pain and loss of control that are associated with disruption in human life and experienced in body and mind … personal struggle and falling apart are signs of strength which enable people to integrate their experiences and change attitudes and patterns of behaviour. Flach suggested that resilient qualities are attained through a law of disruption and reintegration. (Allain-Chapman 2012, p. 24)

This maturing dynamic is seen in the shape of the recovery journey described in Brueggemann's observations about the psalms, Judith Herman's three stages of trauma recovery and the ICTG collective trauma response chart.

Exercising self-compassion, we can face into adversity and struggle, in the process growing into the fullness of our humanity and contributing to the needs of the world.[11] 'Being compassionate toward yourself – not self-indulgent or self-pitying – is both the least you can do and the single most

important thing you can do to make the world a better place'
(Nagoski and Nagoski 2019, p. 211).

Faith, hope and joy

Meaning and purpose are, for many, found in faith traditions
and communities.[12] Studies of highly resilient individuals who
experienced a great deal of adversity show that they have a
moral compass, a belief in something greater than themselves,
they are altruistic and they have mission, meaning and purpose
in their lives (Zimmerman 2020).[13]

Faith – its precepts, traditions, practices and communities – is
a strong resource for meaning. The Bible is a veritable treasure
trove of survivor literature. Meg Warner (2020a) excavates the
story of Joseph in the book of Genesis to illustrate and explore
more deeply the contours of resilience. Allain-Chapman
(2012, pp. 53–6) draws on scripture and tradition to frame the
encounter with adversity as a desert experience. She observes
that meditation and prayer are integrating, creative processes
(Allain-Chapman 2012, p. 28). One of the spiritual practices
that sustained and accompanied my post-traumatic journey
was to sit in church on Sunday mornings, one ear cocked to
the preacher, and write poems that revealed to me where the
lectionary readings were landing in my life (Grosch-Miller
2020).

Our faith resources nourish us for the journey. The stories of
our ancestors give us hope. In his final letter, having endured
numerous adversities, Paul tells us that suffering produces
endurance, which produces character, which produces hope,
which does not disappoint us (Romans 5.1–5a). The love of
God, gift of the Holy Spirit, sustains us in hope. We are not
alone. Others, including our ancestors, have suffered too.
Endurance will get us to God's good end.

Hope is an inner quality, part of the process and product
of resilience. As is joy. Much has been written about the difference between happiness and joy. The first derives from the
good that happens to us; joy, though, happens in us when we

are connected to ourselves and the something larger that gives our lives meaning. It is a barometer for vocation. As Frederick Buechner (1993) says: 'The place God calls you to is where your deep gladness and the world's deep hunger meet.'[14]

Resilience and post-traumatic growth

We are changed by the traumas we experience. Our nervous systems are changed (van der Kolk 2014, pp. 2–3, 21, 347).[15] The story we tell about our life changes, for good or for ill depending on our focus and the conclusions we draw. If we have the good fortune to have had access to the resources we needed and the capability to connect to them, we may come out on the other side potentially stronger and wiser. Recall that the Phases of Trauma chart ends in 'wiser living'.

Post-traumatic growth is a catch-all concept for the positive psychological, emotional and/or spiritual changes that may come as a result of having survived a traumatic experience. Survival is the necessary precondition for the possibility of post-traumatic growth. To survive, there is a need to cultivate and practise resilience.

Earlier I mentioned that there is some evidence that greater adversity has a correlation with greater post-traumatic growth. Researchers have identified five areas in which post-traumatic growth may be manifested: spiritual/existential change; relating to others; appreciation of life; new possibilities; and personal strength (Weber et al. 2019, pp. 266–77). In other words, as a result of surviving adversity we may emerge with a stronger sense of self and capability, a deepened love of life and clarified or renewed relationships and priorities. Allain-Chapman argues that these changes, resourced by faith, have a moral flow – from adversity to altruism.

Accompanying the traumatized individual: dangers and opportunities

As the survivor is the expert, the role of the accompanying pastoral carer is geared towards hearing them into speech as they find their way, respecting the survivor's autonomy and agency, and signposting resources. While the role is clear, the way is still fraught with danger. As discussed in Chapter 7 (Superheroes), anyone who is exposed to the suffering of others is susceptible to vicarious or secondary trauma, compassion fatigue or burnout.

All our caring must be rooted in the same principle that guides the survivor's post-traumatic journey: self-compassion. We can only reliably give what we have. There are necessary limits to what that will be. We have to be ever vigilant about meeting our own needs or we will not be able to be the witness a survivor needs. Accompanying the post-traumatic journey is costly as well as rewarding. Seeing someone survive is gratifying. Seeing them emerge with new capabilities and strengths even more so. Our self-care makes these more possible.

Two psychological concepts help pastoral carers to exercise their ministry as safely and productively as possible. The first is boundaries. Boundaries derive from a fundamental respect for the other and one's own being. But given our pro-sociality and natural identification and mirroring of others, it is easy to get muddled about this. This is particularly true in ministry which does not have the safeguards of other helping professions in regard to training and required supervision, although that is changing. One way to think about boundaries is to ask: *What is my role here? Whose responsibility is it?* A person's healing and growth is their own responsibility. Pastoral carers offer a listening ear, encouragement and support but in the end every person's life is their own responsibility. They are the ones who will have to live it.

The second concept that helps secure the helping role concerns empathy. Warm, resonant care is undoubtedly empathetic care. But there are different kinds of empathy: the kind that preserves the boundaries between survivor and pastoral carer and the kind more susceptible to dissolving it. The first kind can be called *cognitive empathy*. A pastoral carer exercising cognitive empathy draws on their own experiences to connect with what the other person is going through but preserves distance and perspective. A pastoral carer exercising *emotional* or *affective empathy* feels with the person they are caring for, risking entanglement and dissolution of boundaries (Parry 2017a, p. 154).[16]

Caring is a serious business. In tending to the wounds of others we come face to face with our own wounds. We are indeed wounded healers. The dangers, Allain-Chapman (2012, pp. 112–13) observes, include transference and countertransference when our 'stuff' gets mixed up with the 'stuff' of the person we are accompanying, a defended superiority and becoming overwhelmed by pain. Prevention comes with tending to our woundedness, boundary-keeping and limit-setting. We need to manage our own less than helpful proclivities such as the desire to rescue or save another. And we need assiduously to practise the self-compassion at the heart of resilience. Modelling self-compassion may be one of the greatest gifts we can give another.

Self-care and self-compassion together are one of the four factors that have been identified as reducing the risk of being secondarily traumatized in one's caring (Ludik and Figley 2017, pp. 112–23). The other three factors are not surprising, relating as they do to resilience strategies discussed above: detachment (boundaries and maintaining empathy as cognitive), a sense of satisfaction (meaning and purpose) and social support.

Finally, notice when you are in over your head. Most ministers are not trauma therapists. We can do harm as well as good. Know your personal limits and the limits of your role. When they are reached, refer the person for whom you are caring to specialist mental health provision.

Community and congregational resilience

The resilience of a community or congregation both supports and draws on the resilience of individuals. That is why resourcing the resilience of individuals is an important part of recovery from collective trauma, as is doing what can be done to increase the resilience of the group. Consider this analogy for community resilience used by a director of disaster planning:

> I use the analogy of a sheet and the thread-counts of a sheet. If you have a sheet hanging fully taut with a very low thread-count and something is thrown at it, chance is there will be a hole. The size of the hole will be greater the lower the thread count. But the higher the thread count is ... [the] more resistant it is to damage. Each thread represents something that we as individuals or as a group pull upon to make us feel safe, to make us feel happy, to make us express when we don't feel eager to. (Saul 2014, pp. 95–6)[17]

Community resilience models of trauma recovery are discussed above in Chapter 8 (The Hurting Whole). The Three C's of trauma recovery – calm, communication and care – are offered as habits of the heart that build community resilience in good times and bad in Chapter 5 (Care That Heals). The robust resources available to the community of faith are explored in Chapters 10 through 12 (Lamentation; The Bible; Liturgy and Worship).

Here I will focus on congregations and the hope that is the heart of their resilience. Phil C. Zylla looked at a study of congregations which had survived significant adversities (fire, tornado, clergy sexual misconduct, flood).[18] Drawing on James Hopewell's approach to congregational study,[19] Zylla (2013–14, pp. 100–18) offers these four premises about resilient congregations:

1 A resilient community of faith has an 'ethos' of hopefulness and a narrative that evokes a hopeful view of the world.
2 The features of a resilient congregation include patience, communion and perspective.

3 The compelling narrative that fuels a resilient congregation is the resurrection narrative.
4 The particular language of a resilient congregation includes hope-speak, empowerment by God and humility. (Zylla 2013–14, p. 108)

Hope is central to each premise. Patience is an ally of hope and perspective enables hope to reframe adversity. The resurrection narrative offers hope once dashed and now triumphant. Zylla concludes that the essence of the contemporary congregation is to be a witness to hope in an ever-changing, high-stress world, with 'resilience rooted in the greater reality of God's kingdom' (Zylla 2013–14, p. 116).

Considering the Covid-19 pandemic, Christopher Southgate (2021) focuses on creation, the cross and the eschaton to find hope in adversity. God's good creation is an intelligible and consistent world that includes human ingenuity which may rise to meet the challenges of diverse adversities. The eschatological conviction is that the *telos* of the world is the reign of God where there is no suffering, and in the meantime nothing can separate us from the love of God in Christ Jesus (Romans 8.38–39). Finally and paradoxically, the cross is a source of hope: in agony Jesus cries out from Psalm 22. Southgate reflects:

> This is therefore the ultimate validation of that body of poetry [the lament psalms], which holds fearlessly to the conviction that out of whatever depths the sufferer faces, the sufferer can cry to God ... That connection is always available, and can carry all the bitterness of human experience.
>
> ... meaning can be sustained through any human distress by the thought that God in Christ knows every contour of the abyss of suffering, for all has been experienced in the passion and death of the divine Son. (Southgate 2021)

Brueggemann (2014) identifies nurturing hope as one of the three prophetic tasks of religious leadership in the aftermath of devastating events. Looking at the whole of the biblical witness we can take hope from these revelations: First, that God is. Full stop. We are not left to our own devices. Second, throughout scripture God calls human beings to participate in God's work of redeeming the times and enabling the flourishing of all life. That will not end. So long as the church and her people continue to grapple with reality, name and grieve the losses, and nurture hope, we will be the people of God seeking to bring healing and the new day to light.

Imaging resilience: rock, tree, sand dune

The Dutch practical theologian R. Ruard Ganzevoort images resilience strategies in three ways: as a rock that stands firm amid the rushing flow of the river, as a tree rooted in the earth that sways flexibly in the wind, or as a complex of sand dunes that is picked up in the swirl of a storm and deposited elsewhere in a different shape – still a dune complex but completely rearranged.[20]

The images are helpful in conjunction with the lodestone question, *Is it helping or is it hurting?* Having rock-like resolve to live out of a stance of self-compassion makes a great deal of sense. (When the call of God requires self-sacrifice, self-compassion must stretch to embrace that level of self-giving.) The resolve to cling to God in times of trouble brings strength. But the rigidity of resolve may hurt and not help when it is applied to such things as a refusal to admit pain or vulnerability or to face the facts of a situation. Then the pressure will begin to build and even boulders will roll downstream if the current is strong enough. Over time, water and wind reduce the rock to stone, pebble and grain of sand.

The tree is an entrancing way to visualize resilience. Rooted in, connected to and nourished by the resources of the earth, it draws on the strength of others. Dancing with the breeze, it speaks of flexibility and adaptability – core attributes for coping with a terrible thing and its aftermath. When we cannot accomplish something one way, we seek to find another. Yet some winds are so strong that they can uproot the mighty cedar and break the tallest oak. What then?

The sand dune complex. Grains of sand tiny and humble, accustomed to the company of many. The strongest storms on land or sea will move dunes millimetres or miles and yet they are still an array of sand grains. The image of a dune complex, lifted and reshaped, speaks of retaining core identity – the people of God are still the people of God – while and after enduring the tragedies that befall human living. It is an image for the core task of reframing and retelling the story of our lives and our life in God in the greatest of upheavals.

The spiritual stance of the sand dune is one of humility: acceptance of our creatureliness and of the larger forces that impact on our lives. Humility and surrender. Reinhold Niebuhr's 'Serenity Prayer' comes to mind:

> God, give me grace to accept with serenity the things that cannot be changed, courage to change the things which should be changed, and the wisdom to distinguish the one from the other.
>
> Living one day at a time, enjoying one moment at a time, accepting hardship as a pathway to peace, taking, as Jesus did, this sinful world as it is, not as I would have it, trusting that You will make all things right, if I surrender to Your will, so that I may be reasonably happy in this life, and supremely happy with You forever in the next. Amen.[21]

Conclusion

Trauma and tragedy are no strangers to human life. The family of humanity has faced adversity throughout our time on the earth. Looking ahead we see the potential for more as the climate crisis accelerates, the sixth mass extinction of species continues, political and economic structures struggle to adapt to global events (pandemics, conflicts), and whatever else is revealed that threatens the flourishing of life. Our resilience is to be found in love, faith and hope: the embodied love that begins in a still small voice and extends to the whole world, the faith that enables us to bear reality and name and grieve the losses, and the hope that is at the centre of Christian life. God is. We are not alone. God will continue to call and equip us, striding or limping, into the new day.

Key takeaway points

- Resilience is process and product.
- At the heart of resilience is self-compassion.
- Rest, movement, making choices, relationships, and meaning and purpose are resilience strategies.
- Post-traumatic growth is a possibility, particularly where the loss has been great.
- Hope is at the heart of the resilience of the Christian church.
- Resilience can be imaged as a rock (resolve), a tree (rooted and flexible) or a sand dune complex (reframing); each is appropriate in different contexts.

Notes

1 Parry (2017a, p. 154) quotes Paquita de Zulueta, 'Developing compassionate leadership in health care: an integrative review', *Journal of Healthcare Leadership*, 8 (2016), p. 4.

2 Peyton (2017) provides neuroscientific information, exercises and meditations to enable the brain's healing and transform the self-critic to self-compassion.

3 Holland (2020a) is quoting Dr Lucy Hone.

4 See also Allain-Chapman (2012, p. 26), who identifies from the literature that an 'inner-directed locus of control' is a significant resilience factor.

5 Our bodies and brains have been estimated to need to spend 42 per cent of our time resting (Nagoski and Nagoski 2019, p. 168).

6 See Chapter 2, note 10.

7 Holland (2020b) notes that nearly every study of resilience over the last 50 years observes that the quality of close personal relationships is the most significant determinant of resilience.

8 Research on children with Adverse Childhood Experiences (ACE) shows that the factor most predictive of future thriving is the support of at least one stable and committed relationship with an adult, whether parent, caregiver or other (Center for the Developing Child 2015).

9 Jackson (2017, p. 26) quotes Professor Jamie Hacker Hughes, former President of the British Psychological Society.

10 See also Ganzevoort (2009, p. 187), who observes that post-traumatic growth may be more common than PTSD. He notes that 'according to some, growth instead of pathology is in fact the normal outcome of traumatic stress'.

11 Allain-Chapman (2012, p. 30) observes that the direction of growth is towards living well, which includes loving well, considering one's life to be worthwhile and making a contribution.

12 Faith is not the only source of vocation and service where people find meaning. Family or close personal relationships may be a source of meaning, as can be the achievements of capabilities or goals that leave a legacy. It is all about being connected to something larger than ourselves (Nagoski and Nagoski 2019, p. 59).

13 The other characteristics Zimmerman lists are a positive, realistic outlook; accepting what cannot be changed and focusing energy on what can be changed; and a social support system and supporting others. Additional factors that have been identified as contributing to resilience are role models, physical fitness, brain fitness, and cognitive and emotional flexibility. See Warner (2020a, p. 58).

14 See also 'Vocation', *Frederick Buechner*, www.frederickbuechner. com/quote-of-the-day/2017/7/18/vocation, accessed 9.01.2021.

15 van der Kolk (2014, pp. 2–3, 21, 347) describes how trauma recalibrates the brain's alarm system and has numerous impacts on the nervous system.

16 Parry (2017a, p. 154) discusses the work of Paquita de Zulueta in distinguishing between cognitive and emotional empathy.

17 Saul (2014, pp. 95–6) is quoting Kelly Ryan, New York City Department of Health and Mental Hygiene.

18 Nienaber, Susan, 'Leading into the promised land: lessons learned from resilient congregations', *Congregations*, 3 (Summer 2006), pp. 1–7.

19 James F. Hopewell died before his 1987 seminal work *Congregation: Stories and Structures*, Philadelphia, PA: Fortress Press, was completed. Zylla (2013–14) adapts the editor Barbara Wheeler's observations in the Foreword to posit the essential attributes of resilient congregations.

20 R. Ruard Ganzevoort, conversation with the Tragedy and Congregations team.

21 'What is the full text of the original "Serenity Prayer" by Reinhold Niebuhr?', *Reference* (last updated 8 April 2020), www.reference. com/world-view/full-text-original-serenity-prayer-reinhold-niebuhr-5661eb802a2dbacb, accessed 9.01.2021.

Afterword

Living in the Anthropocene – Resilience and Adaptability

I am writing this in mid-January 2021. We are in our third lockdown in the UK. A new, more highly transmissible variant of Covid-19 is sweeping through the country. Of late, daily deaths have numbered over 1,000 (today over 1,500). When will it end?

Today the BBC reported that 2.6 million people have been vaccinated. It is hoped that in a little over a month's time, all people over 70 and those who are clinically extremely vulnerable will have had the opportunity to receive at least one jab. We do not know if those who are vaccinated can still transmit the virus. As for potential new variants, our scientists are confident that vaccines can be re-engineered quickly to meet the challenge. The vaccine is good news. But it is not enough. I confess that I find myself less and less interested in getting 'back to normal'.

The year 2020 was an *annus horribilis* for the human family. But it was not just bad news for us; the earth and other life forms suffered too – 2020 was the year that we achieved the redoubtable distinction of so filling the planet with our stuff that now there is more human-made material on earth than biomass. It was also the year that upper ocean temperatures hit a record high, nearly 47 million acres of land burned in Australia and the Arctic continued to warm at over twice the rate of subarctic lands. Zombie fires in Siberia and Alaska erupted from peatland and permafrost. Violent storms pummelled areas in East Asia, the United States and South America and included a record Atlantic hurricane season. The sixth mass extinction continued to accelerate: species dying out at a rate 100 times greater than the natural evolutionary rate. This mass extinction has human fingerprints all over it.

We are living in the Anthropocene, the first planetary epoch defined by human activity shaping the natural world ... and not for the good. That human well-being is tied to the well-being of the land is a theme that runs throughout the Old Testament: 'there can be no long-term flourishing of one without the other' (Davis 2009, p. 114; 2010). Is it any surprise that by means of a pandemic the land may be trying to, in Hebrew Bible scholar Megan Warner's words, vomit us out (2020b)? The evidence of the Anthropocene is that we have sold our inheritance, squandered our vocation and forgotten that to be fully human is to protect and preserve. For what? Package holidays and more stuff than we can use?

I strongly suspect that 2020 will have been just the first of many *anni horribiles* to come as we continue to reap the consequences of our ways of living.

How shall we live if rolling crises will be our lot for some time? What does resilience look like in the Anthropocene? What is pastoral care when so much is at stake?

Perhaps some of the lessons of the pandemic will prove 2020 to have been a training ground for years to come. We learned and re-learned some basic things about ourselves and the natural world that can serve us well in the future. We learned how vulnerable we are to forces outside of our control. We learned that our lives are interdependent with others and with the life of the planet. (The earth breathed easier when we stopped rushing around: recall the birdsong that was the soundtrack to the first lockdown, the goats that roamed Llandudno freely, the goose that nested in York railway station.) We learned that there can be serious consequences from the simplest of our actions: a handshake or hug can lead to a Covid fatality. But perhaps most of all we learned that we are adaptable. When circumstances require, we do things differently. We create. We innovate. We do what we need to do.

Resilience in the Anthropocene must be rooted in adaptability, and pastoral care must major in strengthening. We are learners our whole lives long, thanks in part to the neuro-plasticity in our brains. The lessons of the sixth century BC, when sustained catastrophe resulted in theological innovation, give me hope. It will not be without pain but we *can* change. We will not survive as a species if we do not. It is clear to me that getting 'back to normal' is not good enough. As Pope Francis (2020) writes, 'This is the moment to dream big, to rethink our priorities – what we value, what we want, what we seek – and commit to act in our daily life on what we have dreamed of.'

Walter Brueggemann's (2014) framework of reality, grief and hope structures the way forward. It will enable us to hear God's call for the living of these days and the redeeming of our time. Facing fiercely into what really is happening in our world, naming and grieving the suffering caused, and holding on to our faith in God who is and who will be and who never lets us go but continually calls us to faithfulness, we will do what we have to do. We will do what we can.

So I end this book on a note of hope. Things are tough. They may well get tougher. But we have all we need to navigate the storms. Getting 'back to normal' has little appeal and, as wonderful as vaccination is and as grateful as I am for it, it is not the answer to our predicament. What is needed today for our tomorrow is what Martin Luther King, Jr prescribed nearly 60 years ago: courage, compassion and creativity. Now, as always, it is about practising the faith, hope and love that engender those qualities.

God help, sustain and bless us and our world in those prac-tices.

Carla A. Grosch-Miller
Northumberland, January 2021

Appendix A

Trauma Response Toolkit

Preparation *prior to* disaster

	Contact name	Contact details
Regional Denominational Head Office		
Church Staff		
Key Church Lay Leaders (including emergency contacts)		
Denominational Media Contact		
Local Police		
Local Disaster Response		
Plumber		
Electrician		

	Contact name	Contact details
Town Councillor/Mayor		
Ecumenical Partners		
Interfaith Partners		
Mental Health Providers (trauma-aware)		
Social Media details (for remote access)		

Put together a resource bag with water, a snack, a Bible, hand sanitizer, tissues, a high visibility vest and this completed form where you can grab it on the way out the door.

During the acute phase

- Take a deep breath; pray – connect to yourself and God
- Discern your role
- Call your regional office; negotiate who will communicate with the media
- Alert your support people
- Call your lay leadership; assemble a response team – what can we offer?
- Identify circles of impact
- Distinguish between urgent and important
- Open the church; rally the troops
- Consider gathering the congregation or the public, in collaboration with other faith community partners and local agencies

- Create an information system
- Check in with church members and others
- Create a press-free zone?
- Care for the carers/consider debriefing for first responders

Remember: This heroic phase will be followed by a difficult period of disillusionment. Pace yourself; make self-care a priority so that you can lead through the days, weeks and months ahead.

After the acute phase

- Watchful waiting as a pastoral strategy
- Welcome honest expression of feelings; don't sugar-coat reality
- Re-establish normal worship and meeting schedule if possible
- Consider whether any special events would be helpful
- Remind congregation we are on a journey that will last some time
- Draw on rich resources in our Bible and tradition
- Care for the carers
- Care for self; arrange supervision or coaching
- Schedule holiday leave

Helpful resources

Tragedy and Congregations Website (UK):
  http://tragedyandcongregations.org.uk/
Institute for Congregational Trauma and Growth (US):
  www.ictg.org/
The Sheldon Hub – doing healthy ministry together:
  www.sheldonhub.org/

Appendix B

Points for Psychological Recovery (Response Pastors Deployment)

Dr Roger Abbott (Response Pastors Advisor)

The following points are for advisory purposes only; they do not come in any particular order of priority, nor should you feel that if you do not experience any of these issues then there is a problem.

Each individual will have their own unique way of reacting to stressful deployments – there is no 'one size fits all'. The human body is more resilient than we tend to think!

While deployed you may well have functioned without any symptoms arising, due to the adrenaline effect which kept you focused and fully functional. Just be mindful that this is not indicative of no symptoms to follow 'down-stream'.

Symptoms to look out for

- Once the deployment is finally stepped down, you may experience unusual tiredness as the adrenaline effect stops – this is natural.
- You may also experience a persistent recalling of events and incidents you have witnessed while on deployment as the brain continues to process naturally. This may affect sleep patterns temporarily.
- Particular instances may become a preoccupation for you, especially where you feel you may have been able to perform better – this phenomenon is not necessarily an accurate guide to how you did/did not perform.

- Your concentration levels at work, or within the home, may become limited – give yourself time and space.
- Your tolerance levels – within the home, at work, or even out-and-about, may be tested severely. You may become more easily irritated for a while!
- You may *feel* that talking about your experience seems pointless.

Actions to take/avoid

- You may judge that you need to adjust your social life temporarily, to give yourself space.
- If at all possible, do not resort to alcohol or medication for relieving the above symptoms.
- When you are ready, talk out your experience with trusted partners/friends who will listen.
- Make much use of prayer, physical exercise and relaxation.
- If possible, do not make critical lifestyle decisions while symptoms persist.
- If symptoms persist for *months*, seek medical advice.

© Roger Philip Abbott, 2017

Appendix C

ICTG Phases of Collective Trauma Response Chart

This chart is heuristic rather than prescriptive, meant to stimulate conversation. Every traumatizing event is different although the flow of the journey to recovery follows a somewhat predictable pattern through these kinds of phases. Recovery may take from two to five years or even longer.

For more information, see the website of the Institute for Collective Trauma and Growth, www.ictg.org/phases-of-dis aster-response.html.

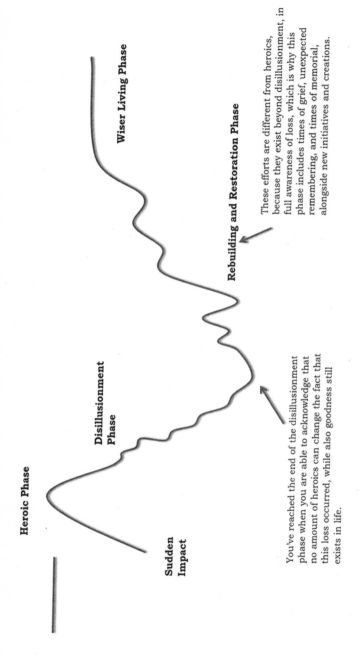

Heroic Phase

Disillusionment Phase

Wiser Living Phase

Rebuilding and Restoration Phase

Sudden Impact

You've reached the end of the disillusionment phase when you are able to acknowledge that no amount of heroics can change the fact that this loss occurred, while also goodness still exists in life.

These efforts are different from heroics, because they exist beyond disillusionment, in full awareness of loss, which is why this phase includes times of grief, unexpected remembering, and times of memorial, alongside new initiatives and creations.

Estimated 24m-60m Community Process

INSTITUTE FOR
COLLECTIVE TRAUMA
AND **GROWTH**

www.ictg.org

Appendix D

A Gathering to Revisit Past Trauma

Looking back to step forward together: a lunch discussion

Six aims drive and shape our work (these were created by the church working group):

- We are aiming to build *cohesion and a common aim* so that we can walk forward together
- We aim to be pastorally sensitive and to foster *care and connection* through the whole congregation
- We aim to *maximize participation* – everyone matters!
- We aim to include an element of *spiritual nurture* in whatever we do
- We aim for *healing* where there has been hurt and *reconciliation* if relationships have been fractured
- We aim to foster *honesty* and to *learn from the past.*

Group covenant for today's discussion:

- Respectful listening without interrupting
- Speaking for oneself, not on behalf of others
- Confidentiality: share the learning, not the stories
- Take responsibility for what you share: if you feel uncomfortable sharing something personal, don't do it.

Outline for the afternoon

Prayer and hymn: 'Brother, Sister, let me serve you'

Lunch, during which facilitators introduce themselves and the group covenant

1–1.15	Input regarding the focus of the event: to express feelings and thoughts about the past event
1.15–2.15	People speak around the tables about the impact of the event on them personally
2.15–2.45	Plenary collection of impressions by table; summary and next steps; prayer.

Please note that X is chaplain to this event. If you would like to speak with them, please seek them out. The sanctuary is also open for quiet time and space.

Appendix E

Facilitator's Checklist

Be Calm, Curious and Connected

Listen to understand what people are thinking and feeling. Make sure everyone has an opportunity to contribute.

Before the event

- Select your table and reserve your seat.
- Are there copies of the handouts with the group covenant on the table?
- Have you had a chat with your co-facilitator about how to back each other up?

At the beginning of the event

- Welcome everyone and introduce yourselves as a facilitator.
- Briefly go over the information on the table handout. Ask everyone around the table if they are willing to abide by the group covenant.

The table discussions

We only have [specify an amount of time] for this so watch the time and gently move the conversation on.

Process reminders:

- *If a person dominates, say:* Thank you for your contributions. I wonder what other people are thinking.
- *If a person is quiet, say:* We haven't heard from everybody. Is there anything anyone who hasn't spoken wants to contribute? We would like to hear it.
- *Normalize difference*: It is entirely normal for there to be many different perspectives in a congregation. Respectful disagreement enables people to grow in emotional maturity, as they are invited to define themselves and stay connected (to be a Me and part of a We). A church makes much better decisions if there are a range of perspectives in the room – if people respectfully disagree with one another.

Your main tools are:

- Self-control (take a breath; think about your role/goals before speaking; if unsure, say so or say little or nothing)
- Calmness
- Clarity about your purpose and role at the table
- 'Say more' – be curious to explore what is behind people's statements
- Summarize: if someone makes a provocative or emotionally evocative statement, after you say 'say more' to seek to understand it, summarize where you think they are: for example, 'So you are concerned that ...'

At the end, the plenary leader will lead from the front, asking each table to report to the larger group, and will then briefly summarize what we have learned and what will happen next.

Appendix F

Lament for a Time of Global Trauma

Most gracious God, Thread of Love that pulses through the earth binding creation to its maker, Light and Life that is our Source and our Breath, we come to you in humility and in need.

We confess that we are terrified. Day-to-day bad news comes across the airwaves to us. Wildfires in California; the melting of Antarctic ice shelves and Arctic tundra; the loss of over two-thirds of the earth's living non-human creatures over the last 70 years and the threat of extinction for more; oceans filled with microplastics; polluted rivers and cities; the trauma of the centuries' old pandemic of racism; crushing poverty for many alongside sickening enrichment of the few; the uncertain impact of Brexit; the chaos and unpredictability of these times.

Why ever did you create a world that we were capable of messing up? Did you anticipate the cost of our precious freedom? Do you weep as you look at the straining, struggling earth you so tenderly crafted and entrusted to us to tend and to till? Are we staring into the abyss of the end of our species' time here? Did you create us just to watch us destroy ourselves? Is your cruelty as great as your love, and how can that be? We toss and turn; we fill our heads with other things to distract us. We do not know where to go or what to do. Is it too late?

You have been our compass and our mainstay for generations. We tell the stories of our ancestors with pride and recall your saving grace in our own lives. Day by day, week by week, we call on you and will continue to do so. But will you answer?

Mighty and merciful God, save us from ourselves. There is no other way. Turn us from our thoughtless consumption, our stuffing our heads and bellies with nonsense that does not nourish, our self-centred prison and narrow horizons. Raise up the leaders we need and help us to heed them. Convert the whole world to the power of self-giving love. Place our feet on the path of right relationship with all the earth and enable us to walk it.

And we will praise you. We will be like those who crossed the Red Sea safely, who journeyed from slavery to freedom, like those who returned home after exile to prepare to rebuild the city. Our mouths will be filled with laughter and our songs will be songs of joy.

Amen.

Carla A. Grosch-Miller, 2020

Appendix G

World Communion Liturgy for a Time of Pandemic

Exodus 20.1–4, 7–9, 12–20; Psalm 19;
Philippians 3.4b–14; Matthew 21.33–46

Call to Worship

Leader: From where we are sheltering in place,
from sacred spaces where
folks are socially distancing themselves,

People: **we are gathered as God's people,**
called to the Table where brokenness
nourishes us with simple grace.

L: From virtual communities all over the world,
with families gathered in living spaces,

P: **we are gathered as God's faithful community,**
serving, living, caring wherever we are.

L: From neighbourhoods made up of those
of every class, every race, every branch of faith,

P: **we are gathered as witnesses to God's hope**
and peace which have not disappeared
in every place, in every person in this uncertain time.

Prayer of the Day

Once, you saw your children
held in bondage by fear and despair
and gathered them up to journey
with them into freedom and hope.

In these days of worry and uncertainty,
continue to walk with your children
who feel captive by a virus we cannot see.
Fill our hearts and souls
with sighs more precious than
all we value, Word Speaker.

Once, you came,
not with blueprints under your arms,
but with grace cradled in your hands.
You came,
not to force us to choose a side
as so many these days try to do,
but to be that voice which calls us together.
You came,
so that we would not have to worry about
what lies ahead of us on these days,
but so we could see that community
of gentleness, of justice, of life you have prepared.
Fill our hearts emptied of hope
with your grace more precious
than our deepest fears, Word Bearer.

When we long to trust those promises
offered to us by those who do not care
for anyone but themselves,
when we are tempted to believe those
who say there is nothing to worry about
and no reason to look out for others,
when we hesitate to put our trust
in those who would have us care
for the forgotten, the most vulnerable,
may we be nudged into seeking
to live out our calling to live in unity.
Fill our uneasy, shattered spirits
with your peace more precious
than the brokenness we grasp, Word of Wisdom.

God in Community, Holy in One,
hear the words of our hearts
as we pray as Jesus has taught us, saying,

(The Lord's Prayer)

Call to Reconciliation

In these confusing days, it is easy to think that there are no rules we need to follow, but we can live, act, do whatever we want. But Paul reminds us that, when we gain Christ Jesus as our Lord and Saviour, we receive exactly what we need – forgiveness, grace, hope. Let us confess our foolishness to God, that we might know God's healing love for us!

Unison Prayer for Forgiveness

If we were to name all the gods we have before you, Rock of Redemption, we would be here for a very long time. We elevate politicians into saviours, though they are as broken as we are. We misuse your name so much during the uncertain and terrifying days, we have trouble speaking to you in prayer at night. We are so busy being worried and fearful, we do not notice how creation witnesses to your goodness and grace.

Forgive us, God our Hope. Even in our uncertainty, may we trust that your love never abandons us. Even in our fears, may we know that your presence never leaves our side. Even when our faith falters, may we know that your grace is the most valuable gift we have, and we can open our emptiness, our hearts, our lives to the healing and loving presence of Jesus Christ, our Lord and Saviour.

Silence is kept

Assurance of Pardon

L: Persistently, patiently, lovingly,
    God pours out grace and joy into our lives,
    healing our brokenness, forgiving our sin.
P: **Loved, we are sent to love those who have been forgotten.**
    Forgiven, we are freed to offer mercy
    to those who are cruel to us.
    Graced, we can offer our gifts to everyone we meet.
    Thanks be to God. Amen.

Prayer of Dedication/Offering

We can join in hoarding all the gifts with which you bless us,
God of generosity, or we can share them with others. May
what we offer in these moments be the very blessing, the very
hope, the very peace others need. This we pray in the name of
Jesus. Amen.

Great Prayer of Thanksgiving

L: May the composer of hope be with you!
P: **And also with you!**
L: Beloved, God has created us to live faithfully in these times.
P: **We lift our hearts to the One**
    who shapes us into communities of grace and peace.
L: Join in singing to God, who takes away all our fears.
P: **We will dance with joy to the Table of peace and hope,**
    even if it is the table in our kitchen or living room.
L: We tremble in these moments
    of uncertainty, of days which seem endless,
    wondering if there is any word for us.
    So, remind us that you spoke
    into the trembling emptiness of chaos,
    and your goodness and wonder
    began all those days and nights
    when hope raced across the sky,

when grace bubbled up from springs,
when peace wandered the meadows.

All these gifts were, and still are,
crafted for those made in your image,
even when we grumble in wildernesses
or live in the exile of fear and worry,
or seek to have our way, not yours.

In every moment when your people
were alone, afraid, felt abandoned by all,
you sent prophets – women and men,
to remind us of your promises and point us
to all the ways you continue to love.

Even in these months of isolation,
even in these days which seem the same,
even in these moments we are alone,
you are with us, in the life, the promises
made known in the Child you sent
to point us to the way home to you.

So, with those who trembled at
the foot of your holy mountain,
and with those who press on to follow you,
we join our voices in praise to you:

P: **Your Word opens our eyes to all creation.**
Your Word is the sweet taste of joy
for empty hearts.
Your Word helps us to endure through every
moment which seems unbearable.
Blessed is your Word who comes in your name.
Hosanna in the highest!

L: Though others mock us for such trust,
we continue to believe that we know
your holiness in the hope you share, God of our hearts,

and we realize how blessed we are
by the grace we have received in your Child, Jesus.

In these times when we wonder
if anyone really cares about us,
he is the One who is your love
poured out for us, each of us.

In these days when bitter voices
would seek to seduce us with anger,
he is the gentle voice which calls
us to trust in your heart broken for us.

In the moments when people seem
not to care for the most vulnerable,
for those most at risk from this virus,
he is the living demonstration
that death has no ultimate power
but that your resurrecting love
is the final word spoken about us.

As we would seek to model his gentleness
and grace in these overwhelming times,
as we try to let his light be revealed in us,
we would speak of that mystery we call faith:

P: **Setting aside all he valued,
Christ became our treasure,
so we might know how precious we are to God.
Setting aside his own life,
Christ rescued us from all foolishness
so we might know the One who loves us.
Setting aside our doubts and fears,
we yearn for the promise of the return
of the grace, love, and hope of Christ.**

L: Now, around table and altars
in sacred spaces which echo with silence,

around nicked and initialized wooden tables
and glass-topped tables in homes,
we pray, Redeemer of all creation,
that you would pour out your Spirit
on each and every place,
and on each and every person.

Whether it is bread that is broken,
or crackers that are split apart,
may these gifts remind us
that it is moments when we least expect,
for those people we usually do not notice,
that we are called
to share your grace,
to listen to the lonely,
to welcome the heartbroken,
to embrace the vulnerable.

Whether it is a mug of tea,
a glass of wine or juice,
or even a glass of water,
may this be your grace poured into us
so that we might become
people who will not give up on justice,
people who will not let go of hope,
people who will not hoard life,
people who will trust in you always.

And when this pandemic comes to an end
and we can gather once again
with our sisters and brothers around the Table,
we will know your promised Feast
in that place, that time, that life beyond this,
where all hurtful words silenced,
where all pain is left behind,
where hope and grace are our closest friends,
and we will join our hearts and voices
with our sisters and brothers

who forever sing of your glory,
God in Community, Holy in One. **Amen.**

Sending

L: Even in this time of pandemic,
    we are a blessed people.
P: **We will go to be a blessing in the world.**
L: Even when there are so many angry people around us,
    we are the face of Jesus.
P: **We will go to be love and compassion to all.**
L: Even when we are isolated, quarantined,
    living in lockdowns, we are the family of God.
P: **We will go to serve our sisters and brothers
    wherever we may find them.**

© 2020 Thom M. Shuman, reprinted with permission.

Glossary of Terms

Adrenaline: a hormone that is released in response to acute stress which acts to increase the heart rate and blood pressure, among other things, and prepares the body to fight or flee.

Amygdala: an almond-shaped cluster of nuclei, one in each hemisphere, near the base of the brain which is part of the limbic system and functions as an early warning system. The amygdala scans the environment every 12–100 times a second for physical or emotional threat. When threat or danger is detected, a rapid-fire signal is sent to the hypothalamus to trigger a fight or flight response.

Autonomic nervous system (ANS): the part of the nervous system that is linked to the internal organs and automatically regulates body functions including breathing, digestion, heart rate and blood pressure, urination and defecation and sexual response. It is the first part ('reptilian brain') of the three-part brain model and develops in utero. It has two main divisions: the sympathetic nervous system and the parasympathetic nervous system.

Cortisol: the primary stress hormone that fuels the body's fight or flight response, increasing sugar in the bloodstream and the enablement of the body to repair tissues while decreasing non-essential body functions or those that would be detrimental to fighting or fleeing.

Enteric brain: the complex system of about 500 million sensory and motor neurons embedded in our gastrointestinal walls from the end of the esophagus to the anus.

Epigenetics: changes in an organism that are inheritable but that do not manifest from a change in the DNA sequence. Such changes may result from environmental, external or normal developmental factors and may affect gene activity and expression.

Felt sense: the information that arises from our enteric brain (gut).

Hippocampus: part of the limbic system, the hippocampus is a complex brain structure that is involved in learning and memory, playing an important part in consolidating information from the short-term to the long-term memory. There is one in each hemisphere of the brain.

Hypothalamus: part of the limbic system, the hypothalamus is triggered by the amygdala to prompt the adrenal glands to release stress hormones including adrenaline and cortisol.

Left hemisphere of the brain: the brain has a left and a right side, the two of which are almost mirror images of each other. They have different structures and specializations but are interconnected and support each other. The left hemisphere apprehends reality in discrete bits, mechanically putting them together to build a picture. Among other things, it specializes in certainty and logical analysis and brings us everyday language and speech, writing and arithmetic. (Note: some people have a right hemisphere that specializes in language.) It processes verbal memory and finding meaning in memory.

Limbic system: the second part ('mammalian brain') in the three-part brain model, the limbic system is involved in emotional, motivational and behavioural responses, particularly those related to social functioning, as well as memory and learning. It includes the amygdala, the hippocampus and the hypothalamus.

Neocortex: the third part ('neo-mammalian brain') in the three-part brain model, the neocortex takes up over two-thirds of the volume of the brain in human beings. It is involved in language, reasoning, sensory perception, abstract thought and imagination.

Neural pathway: a series of neurons (nerve cells) connected together that enables signals to be sent from one part of the nervous system to another.

Neuroplasticity: the ability of the brain to change throughout life, it is the basis of learning. Frequently used neural pathways are strengthened; rarely used pathways are weakened or eliminated. New pathways are created by new activities.

Parasympathetic nervous system: part of the autonomic nervous system, the parasympathetic nervous system manages the body in ordinary situations. It is the 'rest and digest' system, which seeks to conserve and restore the body. It is involved in the freeze or flop-and-drop response to a traumatizing event.

Resonant care: care that is warm and precise.

Right hemisphere of the brain: see left hemisphere. The right hemisphere apprehends reality as interconnected, evolving and animate. Emotions are read in this hemisphere. Among other things it specializes in spatial reasoning, discerning direction or distance and music and art apprehension. It processes non-verbal memory and recollection of perceptual memory.

Sympathetic nervous system: part of the autonomic nervous system, the sympathetic nervous system prepares the body to flee or fight in a stressful situation. It is the 'get up and go' system, increasing the heart rate and widening airways to make breathing easier, as well as enabling strength and utilization of the body's stores of energy while slowing digestion and urination.

Three-part brain: the theory from the 1960s that the human brain can be divided into three parts: the autonomic nervous system, the limbic system and the neocortex. This division, which is a gross oversimplification, is said to reflect the evolution of the human brain – reptilian, mammalian and higher primates – as well as the development of the brain from before birth to adulthood.

Vagus nerve: the vagus nerve wanders through the body, connecting the brain to the heart, lungs, stomach and intestines. One of the vagus nerve's primary functions is to control the parasympathetic nervous system (rest and digest). It connects the enteric brain to the head brain.

Window of welcome: the amount and kind of emotional expression and intention that a person can meet with warmth and understanding and respond to with resonance.

Bibliography

Alexander, Jeffrey C., 2004, 'Towards a theory of cultural trauma' in Alexander, Jeffrey C., Ron Eyerman, Bernhard Geisen, Neil J. Smelser and Piotr Sztompka, *Cultural Trauma and Collective Identity*, Berkeley, CA: University of California Press.

Allain-Chapman, Justine, 2012, *Resilient Pastors: The Role of Adversity in Healing and Growth*, London: SPCK.

Attig, Tom, 2002, 'Questionable assumptions about assumptive worlds' in Kauffman, Jeffrey (ed.), *Loss of the Assumptive World: A Theory of Traumatic Loss*, The Series in Trauma and Loss, 15, New York and London: Brunner-Routledge, pp. 55–63.

Balentine, Samuel E., 2016, 'Legislating divine trauma' in Boase, Elizabeth and Christopher G. Frechette (eds), *Bible through the Lens of Trauma*, Atlanta, GA: SBL Press, pp. 161–76.

Billman, Kathleen D. and Daniel L. Migliore, 2006, *Rachel's Cry: Prayer of Lament and Rebirth of Hope*, Eugene, OR: Wipf & Stock Publishers.

Boase, Elizabeth, 2016, 'Fragmented voices: collective identity and traumatization in Lamentations' in Boase, Elizabeth and Christopher G. Frechette (eds), *Bible through the Lens of Trauma*, Atlanta, GA: SBL Press, pp. 49–66.

Boase, Elizabeth and Christopher G. Frechette (eds), 2016, *Bible through the Lens of Trauma*, Atlanta, GA: SBL Press.

Boudreau, Tyler, 2020, 'Feast or famine: a veteran's reflection on moral injury and recovery' in Kelle, Brad E. (ed.), *Moral Injury: A Guidebook for Understanding and Engagement*, London: The Rowman and Littlefield Publishing Group, pp. 47–58.

Bowie, Fiona, 2006, *The Anthropology of Religion: An Introduction*, Oxford: Blackwell.

Brock, Rita Nakashima and Gabriella Lettini, 2012, *Soul Repair: Recovering from Moral Injury after War*, Boston, MA: Beacon Press.

Brown, Brené, 2018a, 'Strong back, soft front, wild heart', *On Being with Krista Tippett* [podcast], National Public Radio (8 February 2018), https://onbeing.org/programs/brene-brown-strong-back-soft-front-wild-heart/.

Brown, Brené, 2018b, *Dare to Lead: Brave Work, Tough Conversations, Whole Hearts*, London: Vermilion.

Brueggemann, Walter, 1984, *The Message of the Psalms*, Minneapolis, MN: Augsburg Press.

Brueggemann, Walter, 2001, *The Prophetic Imagination*, 2nd edn, Minneapolis, MN: Fortress Press.

Brueggemann, Walter, 2014, *Reality, Grief, Hope: Three Urgent Prophetic Tasks*, Cambridge and Grand Rapids, MI: William B. Eerdmans Publishing Company.

Brueggemann, Walter, 2020, *Virus as a Summons to Faith: Biblical Reflections in a Time of Loss, Grief and Uncertainty*, Eugene, OR: Wipf and Stock Publishers.

Buechner, Frederick, 1993, *Wishful Thinking: A Seeker's ABC*, San Francisco, CA: Harper.

'Care', *Online Etymology Dictionary*, www.etymonline.com/word/care, accessed 9.04.2020.

Carr, David M., 2014, *Holy Resilience: The Bible's Traumatic Origins*, New Haven, CT and London: Yale University Press.

Center for the Developing Child, Harvard University, 2015, 'InBrief: The Science of Resilience', https://46y5eh11fhgw3ve3ytpwxt9r-wp engine.netdna-ssl.com/wp-content/uploads/2015/05/InBrief-The-Science-of-Resilience.pdf, accessed 18.11.2020.

Chalke, Steve, Ian Sansbury and Gareth Streeter, 2017, *In the Name of Love: The Church, Exclusion and LGB Mental Health Issues*, London: The Oasis Foundation.

Churches Together in Britain and Ireland (CTBI), 2002, *Time for Action: Sexual Abuse, the Churches and a New Dawn for Survivors*, London: CTBI.

Clark, Peter Yuichi, 2016, 'Toward a pastoral reading of 2 Corinthians as a memoir of PTSD and healing' in Boase, Elizabeth and Christopher G. Frechette (eds), *Bible through the Lens of Trauma*, Atlanta, GA: SBL Press, pp. 231–47.

Coady, Alanna et al., 2020, 'The emergence and development of the concept of moral injury' in Kelle, Brad E. (ed.), *Moral Injury: A Guidebook for Understanding and Engagement*, London: The Rowman and Littlefield Publishing Group, pp. 21–32.

Cotrill, Amy C., 2020, 'Moral injury and humanizing the enemy in Judges 5' in Kelle, Brad E. (ed.), *Moral Injury: A Guidebook for Understanding and Engagement*, London: The Rowman and Littlefield Publishing Group, pp. 149–60.

Currier, Joseph M. and Wesley H. McCormick, 2020, 'Addressing moral injury in psychotherapy and counseling' in Kelle, Brad E. (ed.), *Moral Injury: A Guidebook for Understanding and Engagement*, London: The Rowman and Littlefield Publishing Group, pp. 97–110.

Damasio, Antonio, 2000, *The Feeling of What Happens: Body, Emotion and the Making of Consciousness*, London: Vintage.

Davis, Ellen F. and Wendell Berry, 'The art of being creatures', *On Being with Krista Tippett* [podcast], National Public Radio (broadcast 10 June 2010, updated 16 April 2020), https://onbeing.org/programs/wendell-berry-ellen-davis-the-art-of-being-creatures/.

Davis, Ellen F., 2009, 'Learning our place: the agrarian perspective of the Bible', *Word & World*, 29.2 (Spring 2009), pp. 109–20.

Dekel, Rachel, 2017, 'My personal and professional trauma resilience truisms', *Traumatology*, 23.1, pp. 10–17.

'Discipline', *Online Etymology Dictionary*, www.etymonline.com/search?q=discipline, accessed 28.04.2020.

Frechette, Christopher G., 2016, 'Daughter Babylon raped and bereaved (Isaiah 47): symbolic violence and meaning-making in recovery from trauma' in Boase, Elizabeth and Christopher G. Frechette (eds), *Bible through the Lens of Trauma*, Atlanta, GA: SBL Press, pp. 67–83.

Frechette, Christopher G. and Elizabeth Boase, 2016, 'Defining "trauma" as a useful lens for biblical interpretation' in Boase, Elizabeth and Christopher G. Frechette (eds), *Bible through the Lens of Trauma*, Atlanta, GA: SBL Press, pp. 1–23.

Ganzevoort, R. Ruard, 1998, 'Religious coping reconsidered, part two: a narrative reformulation', *Journal of Psychology and Theology*, 26.3, pp. 276–86.

Ganzevoort, R. Ruard, 2009, '"All things work together for good"? Theodicy and post-traumatic spirituality' in Gräb, Wilhelm and Lars Charbonnier (eds), *Secularization Theories, Religious Identity, and Practical Theology: Developing International Practical Theology for the 21st Century*, International Practical Theology, volume 7, Münster: LIT Verlag, pp. 183–92.

Griffin, Brandon J. et al., 2019, 'Moral injury: an integrative review', *Journal of Traumatic Stress*, 32 (June), pp. 350–62.

Grosch-Miller, Carla A., 2019a, 'Practical theology and trauma: the urgency of experience, the power of story' in Warner, Megan et al. (eds), *Tragedies and Christian Congregations: The Practical Theology of Trauma*, Abingdon UK and New York: Routledge, pp. 28–44.

Grosch-Miller, Carla A., 2019b, 'Sexual scandals in religious settings' in Warner, Megan et al. (eds), *Tragedies and Christian Congregations: The Practical Theology of Trauma*, Abingdon UK and New York: Routledge, pp. 239–55.

Grosch-Miller, Carla A. (with Megan Warner and Hilary Ison), 2019c, 'Enabling the work of the people: liturgy in the aftermath of trauma' in Warner, Megan et al. (eds), *Tragedies and Christian Congregations: The Practical Theology of Trauma*, Abingdon UK and New York: Routledge, pp. 149–66.

Grosch-Miller, Carla A., 2020, *Lifelines: Wrestling the Word, Gathering Up Grace*, Norwich: Canterbury Press.

Haines, Steve, 2016, *Trauma is Really Strange*, Standing, Sophie (illus.), London and Philadelphia, PA: Jessica Kingsley Publishers.

Harris, Harriet, 'Pastoral care in the time of Covid-19', 24 June 2020, online conference hosted by Trinity College, University of Glasgow.

Herman, Judith, 1992/2015, *Trauma and Recovery: The Aftermath of Violence – From Domestic Abuse to Political Terror*, New York: Basic Books.

Holland, Eva, 2020a, 'In a crisis, we can learn from trauma therapy', *New York Times*, 15 June, www.nytimes.com/2020/06/15/health/resilience-trauma-emdr-treatment.html, accessed 19.11.2020.

Holland, Eva, 2020b, 'What makes some people more resilient than others', *New York Times*, 18 June, www.nytimes.com/2020/06/18/health/resilience-relationships-trauma.html, accessed 19.11.2020.

Ison, Hilary, 2019, 'Working with an embodied and systemic approach to trauma and tragedy' in Warner, Megan et al. (eds), *Tragedies and Christian Congregations: The Practical Theology of Trauma*, Abingdon UK and New York: Routledge, pp. 47–63.

Jackson, Catherine, 2017, 'Picking up the pieces' in *Therapy Today* (September), pp. 24–8.

Janoff-Bulman, Ronnie, 1992, *Shattered Assumptions: Towards a New Psychology of Trauma*, New York and Toronto: The Free Press.

Jones, Serene, 2009, *Trauma and Grace: Theology in a Ruptured World*, Louisville, KY: Westminster John Knox Press.

Kauffman, Jeffrey, 2002, 'Safety and the assumptive world: a theory of traumatic loss' in Kauffman, Jeffrey (ed.), *Loss of the Assumptive World: A Theory of Traumatic Loss*, The Series in Trauma and Loss, 15, New York and London: Brunner-Routledge, pp. 205–12.

Koltko-Rivera, Mark E., 2006, 'Rediscovering the later version of Maslow's hierarchy of needs: self-transcendence and opportunities for further theory, research, and unification', *Review of General Psychology*, 10.4, pp. 302–17.

Kraus, Laurie, David Holyan and Bruce Wismer, 2017, *Recovering from Un-Natural Disasters: A Guide for Pastors and Congregations after Violence and Trauma*, Louisville, KY: Westminster John Knox Press.

Krystal, Henry, 2002, 'What cannot be remembered or forgotten' in Kauffman, Jeffrey (ed.), *Loss of the Assumptive World: A Theory of Traumatic Loss*, The Series in Trauma and Loss, 15, New York and London: Brunner-Routledge, pp. 213–20.

Larson, Duane H., 2020, 'Spiritual formation and pastoral care approaches to moral injury' in Kelle, Brad E. (ed.), *Moral Injury: A Guidebook for Understanding and Engagement*, London: The Rowman and Littlefield Publishing Group, pp. 97–110.

Lawson, Sarah, 2017, 'My self-compassion journey: from striving to sharing satisfaction' in Parry, Sarah (ed.), *Effective Self-Care and Resilience in Clinical Practice: Dealing with Stress, Compassion Fatigue, and Burnout*, London and Philadelphia, PA: Jessica Kingsley Publishers, pp. 112–21.

Layzell, Ruth, 2019, 'Pastoral response to congregational tragedy' in Warner, Megan et al. (eds), *Tragedies and Christian Congregations: The Practical Theology of Trauma*, Abingdon UK and New York: Routledge, pp. 197–210.

Lee, Nancy C., 2010, *Lyrics of Lament: From Tragedy to Transformation*, Minneapolis, MN: Fortress Press.

Lettini, Gabriella, 2020, 'Moral injury and its causes, symptoms, and responses' in Kelle, Brad E. (ed.), *Moral Injury: A Guidebook for Understanding and Engagement*, London: The Rowman and Littlefield Publishing Group, pp. 33–44.

Levine, Peter A., 1997, *Waking the Tiger: Healing Trauma*, Berkeley, CA: North Atlantic Books.

Litz, Brett T. et al., 2009, 'Moral injury and moral repair in war veterans: a preliminary model and intervention strategy', *Clinical Psychology Review*, 29, pp. 695–706.

Ludick, Marné and Charles R. Figley, 2017, 'Toward a mechanism for secondary trauma induction and reduction: reimagining a theory of secondary traumatic stress', *Traumatology*, 23.1, pp. 112–23.

MacLean, Paul, 1990, *The Triune Brain in Evolution: Role in Paleocerebral Functions*, New York: Plenum.

Marques, Luanna, 'Building emotional resilience during the COVID-19 pandemic', online lecture, 11 December 2020, Harvard Club of the UK.

McDonald, Joseph, 2020, 'What is moral injury?: current definitions, perspectives, and context' in Kelle, Brad E. (ed.), *Moral Injury: A Guidebook for Understanding and Engagement*, London: The Rowman and Littlefield Publishing Group, pp. 7–20.

McLaughlin, Ryan Patrick, 2020, 'Lamenting God's good creation', Paper for the Christian Theology in the Midst of Covid-19 online conference, University of Winchester.

Menakem, Resmaa, 2017, *My Grandmother's Hands: Racialized Trauma and the Pathway to Mending Our Hearts and Bodies*, Las Vegas, NV: Central Recovery Press.

Moon, Zachary, 2020, 'Moral injury and the role of chaplains' in Kelle, Brad E. (ed.), *Moral Injury: A Guidebook for Understanding and Engagement*, London: The Rowman and Littlefield Publishing Group, pp. 59–69.

Moltmann, Jurgën, 1974, 'Wrestling with God: a personal meditation' in Moltmann, Jurgën, *The Source of Life: The Holy Spirit and the Theology of Life*, Kohl, Margaret (trans.), Minneapolis, MN: Fortress Press.

Nagoski, Emily and Amelia Nagoski, 2019, *Burnout: The Secret to Solving the Stress Cycle*, London: Vermilion.

O'Donnell, Karen, 2019, 'Eucharist and trauma: healing in the B/body' in Warner, Megan, et al. (eds), *Tragedies and Christian Congregations: The Practical Theology of Trauma*, Abingdon UK and New York: Routledge, pp. 182–96.

O'Donnell, Karen, 2020, 'The voices of the Marys: towards a method in feminist trauma theologies' in O'Donnell, Karen and Katie Cross (eds), *Feminist Trauma Theologies: Body, Scripture and Church in Critical Perspective*, London: SCM Press, pp. 3–20.

O'Donnell, Karen and Katie Cross (eds), 2020, *Feminist Trauma Theologies: Body, Scripture and Church in Critical Perspective*, London: SCM Press.

Palmer, Parker, 2000, *Let Your Life Speak: Listening for the Voice of Vocation*, San Francisco, CA: Jossey-Bass Inc.

Pargament, Kenneth I., Nichole A. Murray-Swank and Annette Mahoney, 2008, 'Problem and solution: the spiritual dimension of clergy sexual abuse and its impact on survivors', *Journal of Child Sexual Abuse*, 17.3–4, pp. 397–420.

Park, Crystal L., 2016, 'Meaning making in the context of disasters', *Journal of Clinical Psychology*, 72.12, pp. 1234–46.

Park, Soyoung Q. et al., 2017, 'A neural link between generosity and happiness', *Nature Communications* (11 July), www.nature.com/articles/ncomms15964.pdf, accessed 27.11.2020.

Parkes, Colin Murray, 2002, 'Postscript' in Kauffman, Jeffrey (ed.), *Loss of the Assumptive World: A Theory of Traumatic Loss*, The Series in Trauma and Loss, 15, New York and London: Brunner-Routledge, pp. 237–41.

Parry, Sarah, 2017a, 'Making space for hope, nurturing resilience and holding on to compassion' in Parry, Sarah (ed.), *Effective Self-Care and Resilience in Clinical Practice: Dealing with Stress, Compassion Fatigue, and Burnout*, London and Philadelphia, PA: Jessica Kingsley Publishers, pp. 149–62.

Parry, Sarah, 2017b, 'Preface: sharing stories as a means of exploring experiences' in Parry, Sarah (ed.), *Effective Self-Care and Resilience in Clinical Practice: Dealing with Stress, Compassion Fatigue, and Burnout*, London and Philadelphia, PA: Jessica Kingsley Publishers, pp. 8–30.

Pattani, Aneri, 2020, 'Sleepless nights, hair loss and cracked teeth: pandemic stress takes its toll', *Kaiser Health News*, for National Public Radio (US), 14 October 2020.

Peyton, Sarah, 2017, *Your Resonant Self: Guided Meditations and Exercises to Engage Your Brain's Capacity for Healing*, London and New York: W. W. Norton & Company.

Pope Francis and Austen Ivereigh, 2020, *Let Us Dream: The Path to a Better Future*, London: Simon & Schuster.

Poser, Ruth, 2016, 'No words: the book of Ezekiel as trauma literature and a response to exile' in Boase, Elizabeth and Christopher G. Frechette (eds), *Bible through the Lens of Trauma*, Atlanta, GA: SBL Press, pp. 27–48.

Rambo, Shelly, 2010, *Spirit and Trauma: A Theology of Remaining*, Louisville, KY: Westminster John Knox Press.

Rambo, Shelly, 2017, *Resurrecting Wounds: Living in the Afterlife of Trauma*, Waco, TX: Baylor University Press.

Ramsay, Nancy J., 2020, 'Spiritual care for veterans and their families affected by moral injury' in Kelle, Brad E. (ed.), *Moral Injury: A Guidebook for Understanding and Engagement*, London: The Rowman and Littlefield Publishing Group, pp. 111–22.

Rando, Therese A., 2002, 'The "curse" of too good a childhood' in Kauffman, Jeffrey (ed.), *Loss of the Assumptive World: A Theory of Traumatic Loss*, The Series in Trauma and Loss, 15, New York and London: Brunner-Routledge, pp. 171–92.

Rolbiecki, Abigail et al., 2017, 'A qualitative exploration of resilience among patients living with chronic pain', *Traumatology*, 23.1, pp. 89–94.

Rothschild, Babette (with Marjorie L. Rand), 2006, *Help for the Helper: The Psychophysiology of Compassion Fatigue and Vicarious Trauma, Self-Care Strategies for Managing Burnout and Stress*, New York and London: W.W. Norton & Company.

Roycroft, Matthew et al., 2020, 'Limiting moral injury in healthcare professionals during the COVID-19 pandemic', *Occupational Medicine*, 70.5 (July), pp. 312–14.

Salzberg, Sharon, 2020, 'Shelter for the heart and mind', *On Being with Krista Tippett* [podcast], National Public Radio (22 October), https://onbeing.org/programs/sharon-salzberg-shelter-for-the-heart-and-mind/.

Saul, Jack, 2014, *Collective Trauma, Collective Healing: Promoting Community Resilience in the Aftermath of Disaster*, New York and London: Routledge.

Scarsella, Hilary Jerome, 2018, 'Victimization via ritualization: Christian communion and sexual abuse' in Ganzevoort, R. Ruard and Srdjan Stremac (eds), *Trauma and Lived Religion*, Palgrave Series on Lived Religion and Societal Challenges, Switzerland: Palgrave-Macmillan, pp. 225–52.

Shay, Jonathan, 1994, *Achilles in Vietnam: Combat Trauma and the Undoing of Character*, New York: Athenaeum.

Southgate, Christopher, 2019a, 'Annotated interview with Sarah Horsman' in Warner, Megan et al. (eds), *Tragedies and Christian*

Congregations: The Practical Theology of Trauma, Abingdon UK and New York: Routledge, pp. 259–74.

Southgate, Christopher, 2019b, 'Trauma and the narrative life of congregations' in Warner, Megan et al. (eds), *Tragedies and Christian Congregations: The Practical Theology of Trauma*, Abingdon UK and New York: Routledge, pp. 122–33.

Southgate, Christopher, 2021, 'Explorations of God and COVID-19', *Perspectives on Science and Christian Faith*, 73.1, pp. 23–32.

Strawn, Brent A., 2016, 'Trauma, psalmic disclosure, and authentic happiness' in Boase, Elizabeth and Christopher G. Frechette (eds), *Bible through the Lens of Trauma*, Atlanta, GA: SBL Press, pp. 143–60.

Stulman, Louis, 2016, 'Reflections on the prose sermons in the book of Jeremiah: Duhm's and Mowinckel's contributions to contemporary trauma readings' in Boase, Elizabeth and Christopher G. Frechette (eds), *Bible through the Lens of Trauma*, Atlanta, GA: SBL Press, pp. 125–39.

Swinton, John, 2009, *Raging with Compassion: Pastoral Responses to the Problem of Evil*, Cambridge and Grand Rapids, MI: William B. Eerdmans Publishing Company.

Tallentire, Liz, 2017, 'Compassion and the self-critic: a life-changing, shared journey of resilience and connection' in Parry, Sarah (ed.), *Effective Self-Care and Resilience in Clinical Practice: Dealing with Stress, Compassion Fatigue, and Burnout*, London and Philadelphia, PA: Jessica Kingsley Publishers, pp. 46–59.

Turner, Victor, 2008, *The Ritual Process: Structure and Anti-Structure*, New York and London: Aldine Transaction.

van der Kolk, Bessel, 2014, *The Body Keeps the Score: Mind, Brain and Body in the Transformation of Trauma*, London: Random House.

Veerman, Alexander L. and R. Ruard Ganzevoort, 2001, 'Communities coping with collective trauma', Paper presented at the conference of the International Association for the Psychology of Religion, Soesterberg, The Netherlands.

'Vulnerability', *Online Etymology Dictionary*, www.etymonline.com/word/vulnerable, accessed 5.01.2021.

Ward, Frances, 2020, *Like There's No Tomorrow: Climate Crisis, Eco-Anxiety and God*, Durham: Sacristy Press.

Warner, Megan, 2019a, 'Teach your daughters a dirge: revisiting the practice of lament in the light of trauma theory' in Warner, Megan et al. (eds), *Tragedies and Christian Congregations: The Practical Theology of Trauma*, Abingdon UK and New York: Routledge, pp. 167–81.

Warner, Megan, 2019b, 'Trauma through the lens of the Bible' in Warner, Megan et al. (eds), *Tragedies and Christian Congregations:*

The Practical Theology of Trauma, Abingdon UK and New York: Routledge, pp. 81–91.

Warner, Megan, 2020a, *Joseph: A Story of Resilience*, London: SPCK.

Warner, Megan, 2020b, 'Resilience in a time of COVID-19 – three biblical models: plague, uncleanness and indigestion', *Crucible* (12 October), https://crucible.hymnsam.co.uk/articles/2020/october/articles/resilience-in-a-time-of-covid-19-three-biblical-models/, accessed 13.01.2021.

Warner, Megan, et al. (eds), 2019, *Tragedies and Christian Congregations: The Practical Theology of Trauma*, Abingdon, UK and New York: Routledge.

Weber, Marcela C., et al., 2019, 'Modeling resilience, meaning in life, posttraumatic growth, and disaster preparedness with two samples of tornado survivors', *Traumatology*, 26.3, pp. 266–77.

Williams, Richard, Jonathan Bisson and Verity Kemp, 2014, 'Principles for responding to people's psychosocial and mental health needs after disasters', OP94, Royal College of Psychiatrists (November).

Williamson, Victoria, Dominic Murphy and Neil Greenberg, 2020, 'COVID-19 and experiences of moral injury in front-line key workers', *Occupational Medicine*, 70.5 (July), pp. 317–19.

Wilson, Hannah, 2017, 'Modelling imperfection and developing the imperfect self: reflections on the process of applying self-compassion' in Parry, Sarah (ed.), *Effective Self-Care and Resilience in Clinical Practice: Dealing with Stress, Compassion Fatigue, and Burnout*, London and Philadelphia, PA: Jessica Kingsley Publishers, pp. 32–45.

Winnicott, Donald, 1971/2005, *Playing and Reality*, London and New York: Routledge.

Wright, Tom, 2020, *God and the Pandemic*, London: SPCK.

Yandell, Michael, 2020, '"Do not torment me": the morally injured demoniac (Mark 5:1–20)' in Kelle, Brad E. (ed.), *Moral Injury: A Guidebook for Understanding and Engagement*, London: The Rowman and Littlefield Publishing Group, pp. 71–81.

Zimmerman, Eileen, 2020, 'What makes some people more resilient than others', *New York Times*, 18 June, www.nytimes.com/2020/06/18/health/resilience-relationships-trauma.html/, accessed 9.01.2021.

Zylla, Phil C., 2013–14, 'Cultivating the resilient congregation: theoretical reflections and constructive proposals', *McMaster Journal of Theology and Ministry*, 15, pp. 100–18.

Index